The Grown Up Gap Year Diaries

The Grown Up Gap Year Diaries

Laura Bloom

VACATION WORK
The Gap Year Experts

This edition first published in Great Britain 2008 by
Crimson Publishing, a division of Crimson Business Ltd
Westminster House
Kew Road
Richmond
Surrey
TW9 2ND

A catalogue record for this book is available from the British library.

ISBN 978 1 90541 033 0

Cover photo: Thai Buddha Statues in Ayutthaya, Thailand,
©Steve Geer/ iStockphoto

Printed and bound by Mega Printing, Turkey

ACKNOWLEDGEMENTS

I am firstly indebted to Gina Hall of Hill Station for offering me such a wonderful opportunity and for agreeing so wholeheartedly that 'gap years are wasted on the young'!

A great many people have shared their gap journals and insights to help create this book. Special thanks for their generosity of time and spirit are due to Sue, Fran, Tim, Susan, Polly, Ajay, Kate and Keith, Mary-Ann and Michael, Gilly and Ken, James and Linda, Barry and Jean, Paul, Josh, Emrys, Joanne and George, Abby, Charles and Elize, Alex, and Ron.

A small bunch of people helped to make my trip truly magical. I would like to make a special mention of all at Floressa tours, Indonesia and especially Imam Widodo, Mr Piter and the Ngadha people of Boloji, Flores. I was also deeply touched by the hospitality of Sultana Ratu Dalem Hj Sri Mulya, Cirebon, Java. Thanks also to my uncle, Paul Witsenburg, for his insights into our family history.

Once again many thanks to Roni and all at White Ladder Press for giving me the rare opportunity to turn a private gap journal into something more helpful to prospective gap travellers.

I am grateful to Mintel for permission to quote from *Travel and Tourism Analyst – Gap Year Tourism (Mintel, July 2005)*.

Finally, thanks to all who joined me on the road and helped turn an adventure into a celebration: Marijke, Lorraine, Chris, Lucy, David and Laurence. Also for reading the manuscript and offering kind and helpful suggestions I doubly thank Laurence, Marijke and David.

CONTENTS

INTRODUCTION

Do you spend your days staring out of the window wishing you were far, far away from the daily humdrum and the British winter? Are you powerfully aware of time passing by while your dreams of travel and new experiences remain unfulfilled? Perhaps you have always promised yourself a really special break, not just a fortnight's holiday, but time to be you, to explore different cultures and whole fascinating continents. You may have a long-held desire to help out in less developed countries or to explore unique cultures before they disappear. Or after a lifetime devoted to work and family you have promised yourself the time of your life sampling anything from white-water rafting to that unhurried cocktail beside an exotic view. You may not have put a name to this urge, but you long for a grown-up gap year. And so did I.

We are not alone – the consumer research group Mintel has found that as many as a staggering 7.5 million UK workers a year consider a career break. Almost half a million actually take the plunge, representing the world's biggest gap year market. Some are workers in their 30s and 40s, who either resign or negotiate a career break to refresh their spirits in the middle of their career. The other growing market is the over-55s who take off to see the world every year, gaining the nickname SKI-ers – Spending the Kids' Inheritance.

But even if you can afford it, have you got the nerve just to take off? It took me a fair amount of courage to leave my home and head out to the unknown. A successful trip needs planning, organisation and a certain amount of daydreaming over maps. I had so much to consider: should I just buy an open ticket or meticulously pre-book every hotel and side-trip? What should I do about my car and those I was leaving behind? And what on earth should I pack in these days of restricted weight limits?

The Grown Up Gap Year Diaries is an account of my own 85-day trip prompted by a surprise opportunity to take a round-the-world flight. It was an extraordinary experience, and one that has broadened my horizons forever. However, this book is not designed as a comprehensive guide to taking your own grown-up gap year. That topic is covered by the excellent *Gap Years for Grown Ups* (Susan Griffith, Vacation Work 2008). But I hope that it will give you inspiration for your own dream gap year, whatever length of trip or type of experience you hanker after. I also hope that you can learn from my experiences and the experiences of the many other grown-up gappers, whose journals I plundered along the way.

I wanted to know what prompted taking a long trip and the practical steps they took before leaving the UK. What were the highlights of their trip – and the low points? What did they wish they had known before travelling? And how did it feel to come home as a changed person when life had trundled on as usual in their absence? Together, we've gathered a lively and quirky pool of information on how it really is on the grown-up gap trail – and not just how the glossy brochures will tell you it is. The hints and tips that I picked up along the way appear at intervals throughout this book.

It has surprised and gladdened me to find that the grown-up gap year is not about conspicuous consumption or designer destinations. The travellers I spoke to embarked upon their trips as thoughtful endeavours to discover the world and themselves in the process. A few individuals undertook outstanding charity work and most strived to engage with and learn about local communities. Almost all came back feeling younger, fitter, more open to life and having achieved their purpose. Many used the time away from home for reflection and talked about moving towards another more positive stage of their life.

So, you've picked up this book and are wondering if you could really pull all the strands together: time off, budget, itinerary, visas and tickets. You want to know how other travellers created an escape plan and what 'life on the road' was really like. I hope this book answers those questions. I have aimed to give you a foretaste of both the challenges you may face as well as the moments of sheer exhilaration lying ahead. Simply by picking up this book you really have taken the first step on an exciting journey. It's up to you now to achieve your dreams of discovery and travel. Good luck and bon voyage!

OFF THE EDGE

Day 1 Chester, England 2.30am

It was 2.30am on a bitterly cold October night. As two alarm clock bells drilled into my consciousness, I felt the tingle of fear shoot through my exhausted limbs. I groped through the darkness and snapped on the blinding light. I was about to leave my own comfortable home, my dear husband and beloved duvet for three whole months. There were final checklists to be ticked off, passport, money and tickets to be inspected one last time and emotional goodbyes to be said. Pulling on my summer travelling outfit it looked plain ridiculous under the harsh electric light: trekking sandals, bare legs, allegedly crease-free skirt and khaki shirt and my one warm item, a zip-up fleece. My heroically wakeful husband Laurence was up and about, ready to take me to the airport for a 4am check-in.

'Now have something to eat,' he coaxed. Tears made the little plate of lovingly buttered toast float before my eyes.

'I can't. I feel sick.'

What was I doing? Why would any sane woman deliberately fly off into this chilly night on her own (to *Africa* for goodness sake) and cut herself off from home and loved ones for three months? Because you can, came the brave traveller voice inside me. Because the whole wonderful world is out there and you've always wanted to do this.

I suppose we all have a braver self inside us and mine was the smart figure of a sophisticated woman travel writer, complete with black Jackie O sunglasses, a notebook, an all-knowing British tone that rapidly commandeers the best rooms and eager porters, and a first-class railway ticket. This capable woman doesn't let fear get in the way of observing fabulous sunsets from the rims of smoking volcanoes or swapping recipes with bone-pierced tribeswomen. This writer woman doesn't struggle to hold back the tears as the car pulls out of the drive and she gets her last glimpse of the peaceful, sleeping village she calls home.

I had planned to stay positive on the journey to the airport. After all, I wasn't going to see Laurence for months and did want to leave a reasonably sane and attractive impression. It was the bag that blew it. A month earlier, Laurence had rung me excitedly from one of those cut-price supermarkets that have metal trays heaped with bursting packets of socket kits, Chinese needlework sets and one furious person chucking things through the till.

'I've found the perfect bag for you. It's a rucksack on wheels. With a daysack in the front.'

'How much is it?' I was wary already.

'30 quid. But it's full of pockets, really strong and just the right size.'

It was his sheer loving kindness in going off to search for the perfect bag that made me buy it. Not the bag itself, of course. The bag was sky blue nylon and too cheap, which made me instantly suspicious. It was also small, a fact that had been proved during my final day's packing frenzy. It was currently packed as tight as an overpacked parachute bag, despite the vast pile of items that just didn't make it inside before the zips started straining.

'I haven't even got my Pacamac,' I suddenly wailed into the dark silence of the car. Goodness, I wanted to be bright and perky and positive but now, on top of everything else, I had to hope it wouldn't rain anywhere in the whole of the tropics all winter. That's the same winter that's otherwise known as the rainy season. And I couldn't even buy one because I had no room – no room at all – for even a tightly folded paper handkerchief.

We kissed our farewells, shivering on the airport kerbside and Laurence took a photo that revealed me as white-faced with the sort of wild-eyed grin you might produce before making a horrific bungee jump. Because that's how I felt. Like I was standing on the edge of a precipice. I had a kind of bungee harness, of course. I had tickets, I had plans, I had my Monster Itinerary. But however safe and secure all the trappings were, I was on my own jumping into the chasm. And I was about to find out in the next few hours that even a meticulous pre-booked itinerary is no guarantee against going into freefall.

I checked in for the 6am to Amsterdam from where I'd get my first long-haul flight to Nairobi. Then I scuttled off to the empty loo, my nervous tum now boiling like a cauldron. Why was I doing this? Shivering on the icy loo in my thin summer clothes I tried to resurrect the poised and confident travel writer inside me. I got up and slapped bronzing powder on my pasty face and boldly stuck my designer sunglasses up on my head. So what if it was 5.15am in wintry Manchester? Checking my tickets I reeled off the first page of exotic names: Nairobi, Zanzibar, Dar es Salam, Cochin, Jakarta. I was going because it would be a great adventure. Surely when the sun came out I'd laugh at this pathetic beginning? I was going to have such an incredible time – well, here's hoping I was. Another cramp twisted in my stomach. If I could just get my bowels under control, that is.

What is a grown-up gap year?

So where did this urge for the older traveller to take off and see the world come from? People have been taking long journeys as an important stage of their lives since medieval folk marched off on pilgrimages and milords travelled Europe on the Grand Tour. Now gap years taken by young people before or after university have become synonymous with gaining maturity through challenge and valuable time away from mum, dad and teachers. It's not surprising that the older generation want a piece of the action. Firstly, they have the motive. Thousands of grown-up travellers have seen their own friends, families and children return sun-bronzed and super-confident from everywhere in the world from Machu Picchu to Mumbai. They've heard how cheap it is, how thrilling the sights are and how easy it is to hop on a few planes and wake up in exotic places only glimpsed in films and documentaries. From listening to their children's amazing adventures over piles of mud-caked laundry it's a small leap to thinking – maybe I could do that?

Secondly, they have the means. The over-50s are now the wealthiest consumer group in Britain. They have benefited from free education, free health services and never-to-be-repeated pensions. The vast majority have their own home, no mortgage and multiple zeros of equity. And if working, many have jobs that allow generous sabbaticals and career breaks. Their own parents saved all their cash in the bank – and then died. Many parents never got around to that cruise they promised themselves all their working lives. And so, the next generation argue, what's the point of keeping all their savings for their own kids to squander? After all, the kids have already had a great time jetting off around the world. You may have heard the phrase SKI-ing – Spending the Kids' Inheritance. From travellers I've met there's a lot of SPA-ing going on as well – Spending Parents' Assets.

Even more extravagant are gappers in their 30s and 40s. Some missed out on travel because of the daily grind of study and careers in their teens and 20s. But like a raucous wake-up call, successive birthdays remind them time is passing. Tired of all work and no play, they are keen to cash in their savings and legacies and abandon Britain for months at a time. New career break policies mean a job can be kept on hold for a year but in fact many travellers choose 'Resignation Today, Tomorrow the World'. For others, the wish to make a small difference in the developing world is a catalyst to pack up and experience a very different but rewarding lifestyle.

A gap experience can in fact be anything from a couple of months to a couple of years. It can include visiting far-flung family members, volunteering to work for charities, taking part in sports and outdoor activities and indulging in exotic sightseeing and exploration. In fact, it's as inspired as your dreams and as big as your budget.

Mintel, the consumer research company, has found that retired travellers spend more than their university counterparts, with an average spend of £5,000. Career gappers in their 30s and 40s get through even more, averaging a total of £6,000–£9,000. When you are past the first flush of youth, there are issues like comfort to consider, the quality of tours and even the indulgence of flying business class. This is unlikely to be a budget holiday – there is a whiff of indulgence in the air and a sense of payback time for all those years spent working or rearing the family.

OUR GAP YEAR TRAVELLERS

The group of real life gappers I talked to are a mixed bunch who all took the plunge for very different reasons. They have all lent me their diaries and answered lots of frank questions about why they went and what actually happened. What were their high and low points? Did they get sick or have an accident? What new things did they try or learn? Did they meet the locals? And how did it feel to go home?

Fran, 70, discovered an unfulfilled dream at a women's group and set off on her to own to explore it on the other side of the world.

'I wanted to see the world and celebrate being who I am.'

Charles, 58, and Elize, 55, are two luxury-lovers who took a honeymoon cruise and extended tour around India.

'We wanted to see India before it changes for ever.'

James and Linda, both 37, were ready for adventure when an inheritance funded a round-the-world trip.

'We had always talked about going. We both love travelling and hate work!'

Sue, 60, left her husband at home while she celebrated her retirement exploring the Antipodes.

'I had never been alone with only myself to consider and wondered how I would feel.'

Abby, 42, wanted to tour eastern Europe by train – and set off alone when her friend couldn't make it.

'After the end of a bad relationship I needed a change of direction. Travel is a great healer.'

Ajay, 63, is a redoubtable doctor who has taken many trips far off the beaten track including a tour of controversial Burma.

'There is a whole wonderful world out there to see and experience.'

Joanne, 50, and George, 29, are a mother and son who fate sent backpacking together.

'I wanted to celebrate giving up work and my improved health.' Joanne

'Most days in Britain, I thought 'Is this it? Surely there must be something better out there?'' George

Mary-Ann, 43, and Michael, 49, are travelling to find the perfect retirement home by the sea.

'If you don't look you won't find.'

Polly, 53, is an extraordinary textile designer whose enthusiasm and skills have benefited projects in South Africa.

'I wanted new experiences. I just had the travel urge.'

Paul, 31, was depressed by his prospects in Britain so took a year out in Australia.

'I had come to the realisation that life is too important to waste.'

Gilly, 64, and her husband Ken had considered emigrating when younger – would New Zealand still fulfil their dreams?

'It was a lifelong ambition to see the wonders of New Zealand.'

Susan, 45, took her two young sons on an incredible trip around the world.

'I wanted to give my two young sons the experience of backpacking and visit parts of the world before they are destroyed forever.'

Kate and Keith, both 40, are two pleasure seekers who planned to take two years off after an inheritance freed them from work.

'We wanted to break the circle and explore — and see what happened.'

Josh, 47, a personal trainer, had long felt the lure of Asia when he set off to experience life in the raw.

'After burnout in a high-stress role in London I realised that time out was the answer.'

Tim, 54, sold his boat, got in his campervan and headed for Morocco.

'It was time to think of me, to be selfish, after spending a life thinking of everyone else first.'

Barry, 66, and Jean, 61, are serial travellers who follow the sun and cricket all around the world.

'We wanted to get away from the English winter.'

Emrys, 42, has skills that helped him form a charity and spend two years in Ghana working on projects.

'I wanted to do something useful in sub-Saharan Africa.'

It can even make sense to spend a large sum and avoid Inheritance Tax says Charles, 58, a financial adviser who took a long luxurious trip to India:

> 'Giving your savings to your travel agent rather than the Treasury can make sense. Older people forget that above the current Inheritance Tax threshold of £300,000, if they die they will be giving away their fortune at the rate of 40%. A hugely stimulating and luxurious once-in-a-lifetime trip can make perfect financial sense.'

Most of our travellers had sufficient savings to fund their trips. Even those who didn't have savings in the bank did have the resources to raise money from property or hard work. Josh's strategy was to work even harder for a year so he could save enough cash to live in Asia for as long as his cash would last:

> 'On top of my job I worked evenings and weekends on a web design project for a friend's company. At the end I had an extra £3,000 cash in the bank.'

On the other hand, Kate and Keith reflect property boom Britain, with two houses to sell and a legacy at the start of their trip:

> 'We plan on travelling for two years using the money my parents left me to do it. I thought it would be a use they would be proud of – better than paying off the mortgage. The advantage of having a mid-life crisis gap year is that you have a lot more cash to blow.'

Fortysomethings Mary-Ann and Michael combined a legacy with working extra hard for nine months to fund a long trip to Sri Lanka in search of a perfect beachside property. Mary-Ann works as a temp to fund a lifestyle that allows for long periods of travelling.

> 'Our parents have all gone now and Mick's father never got to spend his money on travel. We don't want to make the same mistakes of saving all our lives and then dying soon after retirement.'

THE FACTS: Funding the trip

Most grown-up gappers use the opportunity to spend a chunk of their savings. But if you don't have a nest egg, consider using your assets to raise the extra cash:

- Skills – find extra work on top of your existing job or pension
- Property – let your house to tenants or remortgage your home for a lump sum
- Goods – sell unwanted assets such as cars, furniture or other valuables
- Goodwill – fundraising, for example if benefiting a charity through sponsorship
- Energy – apply for schemes such as VSO (Voluntary Services Overseas) involving paid flights to work in developing countries (www.vso.org.uk)
- Ingenuity – cut back on expenses like meals out, subscriptions and other treats
- Birthdays and festivals – ask for gift vouchers and cash towards the trip

Do, however, beware of getting into debt. It is better to scale down your plans than come home to financial difficulties.

Retirement pensions are of course another spur to turn long-cherished plans of travelling into reality. Even small sums can fund an astute traveller for lengthy periods. In 2006, Sue, aged 60, decided to set off on a five-month trip without her husband.

'After working and bringing up three children I wanted some "me time". I cashed in two tiny pensions as lump sums. I wanted to experience the life of the people rather than be a tourist.'

Tim, on the other hand, had a rocky road to his departure for Morocco:

> '*I had recently sold my business and lost all my capital. To fund the trip I sold my boat.*'

So how did I end up taking my own grown up gap year?

My own trip started life as a vague fantasy. Freedom from the British winter loomed large, culminating in a vision of myself meditating alone on a beach of stunning beauty. Something like the movie *The Beach*, but without the gangs, guns or even Leonardo DiCaprio. Nothing to do but saunter between a yoga pose on the sand and the crystal-clear water. I realise now that this is just an anti-stress fantasy that most workers, parents and all-round busy bees imagine as pure relief from the mayhem that is modern life. Oddly enough, when most people get the chance to travel long term, very few opt for such a lazy agenda. Most travellers immediately realise the true potential of time away without work or responsibilities. There are countries to see, people to meet and experiences to be had. Part of the fun is deciding just how to fill that blank sheet with the hand-picked experiences of a lifetime.

My own fantasies became reality thanks to an internet competition. Always on the lookout for adventure, I came across a website offering a Grown-up Gap Year in the form of a round-the-world flight ticket, a short break in Sri Lanka and a few hundred pounds. 'Where would you go and what would you do for your grown-up gap year?' they asked. It was a good question, and sitting on a beach meditating was hardly going to impress the judges. In fact it was a question that excited my mind so considerably that I had to delete lots of wordy fantasy to get my answer down to the 200-word limit.

Key to my answer were observations of backpackers I'd made on holidays. I had seen a certain breed of British youngster running up huge credit card bills, eating at the local McDonalds, getting drunk at backpacker bars and generally being ripped off by the locals. Gap years are wasted on the young, I wrote. They have no appetite and no appreciation. You need experience of life to really ingest the opportunities that time away offers. I would go to places I had always longed to visit: Indonesia, Africa, India and New Zealand. I would eat and cook and savour the spices and the sights. I would write and recycle my experiences. There was nothing about sitting meditating on a beach.

Naturally, I was trying to impress, but I was also indulging another fantasy. Me as that intrepid solo travel writer in the Jackie O shades, laying a battered notepad on a crisp restaurant tablecloth beside an exotic ocean. Even as I tapped the keys I knew it was a bit of a bluff. But then again, it was only an internet competition. I clicked on Send and rapidly forgot all about it.

It was Christmas Eve and I was up to my elbows in giblet stock when I took five minutes out of the kitchen to check my emails. 'Congratulations!' shrieked the email. 'You are the Grown-up Gap Year Winner.' I can honestly say I felt sick. Downstairs I could hear my as-yet innocent husband chatting away to the family. I love my husband very deeply and rapidly realised I might have done a very shallow and foolish thing. After all, I am 46, very happily married and adore my home and family. I read the email again, with its details of a backpack and sleeping bag they were sending me (no please, not a sleeping bag) and a request for my itinerary. Shakily, I went downstairs and confronted Laurence.

'I've won a round-the-world trip,' I quavered. His face lit up. 'For one person,' I mumbled. He looked crestfallen. 'But maybe you can come for part of it,' I added weakly and covered my cringing face in my hands. My son Chris, over from his new home in New Zealand, was more upbeat. 'That's fantastic, Mum,' he said, hugging me. 'We can get together in New Zealand. If I can get some time off work,' he added, more realistically. So at least I've got a ticket to New Zealand, I consoled myself. And I might get to see Chris for a few days. Maybe I can just have a few stopovers on the way and I can forget all this intrepid traveller stuff.

That was my first reaction. But once the New Year dawned, the braver part of me started to surface. I could go *anywhere*, I mused. That simple word rang in my brain like exotic chimes ringing out from a mysterious Himalayan retreat. I could go *anywhere*. So of course I began to choose a whole list of somewheres – somewheres that sounded exotic, challenging and beautiful – to discover and experience for myself.

WHERE IN THE WORLD?

Once Christmas was over I started to play around with my itinerary. I read the travel sections in the newspapers more carefully and ordered brochures. Travel exhibitions were the perfect day out, with their mix of small travel agents and presentations from the big adventure-tour operators. I also scoured the internet and asked people about the best trips of their lives. Most thrilling of all, I got out maps. Mercator's Projection of the world, with its image of the United Kingdom at the centre, kept me spellbound. I had my free stay in Sri Lanka to factor in, but apart from that I could go anywhere. *Anywhere.*

Unfinished business

Many travellers mention 'unfinished business' in their choice of destination. Fran still smarts about the trip to New Zealand she had to shelve back in the 1960s when her mother forbade her to go:

> *'When I was 21 I had a nursing job to go to in Christchurch but my dad had died when I was 16 and my mum didn't want me to go. Of course in those days when one of your parents said no, you didn't do it.'*

It may be nearly 50 years ago but the motivation to travel around the globe and see the place that might have been her home still burned strongly enough for Fran to book her flights and buy a *Rough Guide to New Zealand* – aged 70.

Gilly and Ken had also considered emigration and spent a lifetime thinking about New Zealand before fulfilling their lifelong ambition.

Josh also had unfinished business after a job teaching EFL (English as a foreign language) in Japan fell through:

> *'I never forgot the excitement I felt when preparing to enter that alien culture. Japan was near the top of my list when I planned my dream itinerary.'*

For Sue, the advent of email had brought about renewed contact with cousins in Australia:

> *'While writing to my cousin I commented that I would love to take the boys to see the Great Barrier Reef and tropical rainforest. For a few days I brooded on how I could achieve this. There the seed lay dormant.'*

Indonesia is my piece of unfinished business, the one place I have longed to visit all my life. My Dutch mother was born on Java, as were her ancestors who travelled out from Holland in the 1760s. All my life I'd heard about its exotic beauty: the old plantations, steaming volcanoes and ruined temples in the jungle. But meanwhile all the news from Indonesia had always been bad: earthquakes, bombs, eruptions, landslides and tsunami of varying size and devastation. Indonesia is also the world's largest Muslim republic with a reputation for anti-western feelings. Looking at the Foreign Office's 'traffic light' warning system it has an orange alert – no travel to some parts and proceed with caution to the rest. No British tour operators currently offer holidays to Java and there are no direct flights to the island's capital, Jakarta. Yet if I don't go now, with a free airline ticket, I am sure I never will. And being in Asia, it will be cheap. I decide I have to fulfil my dream, whatever the scary headlines.

LAURA'S TIPS: Deciding where to go

✓ Make a dream list. Brainstorm and play around with ideas.

✓ Weed out low-priority destinations. For example, Europe is cheaper to visit using no-frills airlines.

✓ It makes sense not to overload your ticket with lots of difficult, short-stay side-trips.

✓ Draft an itinerary. Factor in a rough direction — for example, eastwards around the world.

✓ Consider key dates — start date, festivals, tours, meet-ups with friends and relatives.

✓ Check visa requirements at www.thamesconsular.com or www.trailfinders.com for both application times and allowed length of stay.

Some grown-up gappers will of course know immediately where they want to go. It may simply involve buying a return air ticket, buying a campervan or booking a tour. Others may choose to take trains, sail on a cruise or a freight ship or even cycle or walk. But for many, the option of a round-the-world air ticket expands even the most modest holiday plan into the journey of a lifetime.

Sometimes the excitement simply takes over. Kate and Keith began with the certainty that they would travel for two years with a first stop in South America:

> 'We thoroughly researched our South American trip, knew exactly where we were going, what we would be doing, and then booked a ticket to Bali, Australia, New Zealand and Asia. We were surfing the net and came across a really cheap flight – had a couple of glasses of wine and thought yeah let's do it! We can do South America next year.'

THE FACTS: Visas

- Draw up a list of visa requirements for each country you intend to visit. Be aware that some countries will turn you back without a valid visa.

- As a general rule get as many visas as you can before you leave to avoid wasted time on your trip.

- If this isn't possible, get a general idea of where and to whom you need to apply overseas and pack plenty of passport photos (two to four per country).

- Be aware that some visas count down from date of issue while others only count down from the date of entry.

- Visa rules also vary depending on whether you arrive by air or cross an overland border.

- Fees and rules fluctuate so always check the embassy or consulate just before you send your application.

- Immigration officials may also ask for evidence of onward travel (flight ticket) and sufficient funds – a credit card is generally sufficient.

Visa problems can be a real worry. A few days before travelling to Sri Lanka, Mary-Ann and her partner Michael realised they were heading to overstay on their visa:

> 'Our flights are one day over the 90 days we're allowed on our visa. We've tried to change the flights but we can't. I can't find out if it will be fine when we get to the airport, if we'll just have to slip an official some baksheesh or whether we really will be in trouble.'

I decided to save money by organising my own visas. For example, the cost of obtaining a visa for Kenya from a visa agency is £55. I saved around £20 by downloading a form from the internet (www.kenyahighcommission.net) and sending it by registered post to the Kenyan Embassy with my passport, a £30 postal order (cheques are not accepted) and a couple of photos. The important factor is having plenty of time, although anyone with a few free days and easy access to the embassies in London (and a tolerance for queuing all morning) could sort out most visas independently. Once my passport was returned by special-delivery post, I used it to save my next £25 by sending off for my Indian visa. After investigation I opted to get my Tanzanian visa at Zanzibar airport on arrival, saving £13 on the postal visa and £38 on the fee charged by a visa agency.

Seasons

Seasons are a further factor that I had to consider. In this age of global warming the world's weather patterns can appear fairly random but there are still underlying patterns across the globe. Monsoons, floods, tornadoes and extreme heat or cold are all well worth checking out for before booking. Rain, in particular, can bedevil the best-laid tours in many developing countries, clogging up roads with mud and creating spontaneous new rivers. Trips centred on any activities like trekking, cycling and climbing need to pay special heed to weather patterns. Many global travellers also choose to stay within a single weather zone such as the tropics to aid acclimatisation and cut down on packing.

Local information can prevent a wasted journey to places where environmental conditions could ruin all enjoyment. Kate and Keith were due to go to Laos:

'We had planned to go to Laos but the timing was terrible – the farmers were burning off in the north of Thailand and the pollution was like nothing I had ever come across (and that is coming from a Teessider of 20 years!).'

Viewing wildlife that moves with the seasons will also have an influence on your itinerary and may require extra time. Jean built extra time into her and Barry's stay in New Zealand to see the wildlife:

'We knew that to see the whales at Kaikoura we needed to allow extra days in case boats were cancelled. Good weather on shore doesn't mean the boats go out as it can be very rough at sea.'

Talking to a travel agent

At this point nobody should even think of making any arrangements themselves. Unless you only have one or two destinations, you need a specialist travel agent to book your tickets. Why? There are so many deals, routes and airlines cross-hatching the globe that a single individual can easily waste precious time and money hunting down and failing to catch the best deal.

Sue's impulse to take her two boys around the world resulted in booking her flights at barely a week's notice. She had to hurry to allow for most of the trip being in the boys' school holidays plus an authorised extension. Once she spoke to an agent her original ideas had to be trimmed down significantly:

'The girl I dealt with advised me against our planned itinerary for several, now obvious, reasons. Firstly we had planned too many stopovers and our route exceeded the 29,000-mile limit on a Star Alliance ticket, unless I wanted to pay the surcharge. I didn't. She also advised that if we travelled in a clockwise direction, the effects of jetlag would be minimised, something that had not occurred to me at all. When it came down to it we had to go with the flights we could get.'

THE FACTS: Round-the-world tickets

- Ideally start planning your trip about 12 months before your departure date. Your perfect round-the-world itinerary rarely gets cheaper – it just gets full.

- Departure dates are often fixed but onward legs can sometimes be changed for a fee.

- Name changes can be expensive – think hard about your ticket name if getting married or before buying a ticket for a fickle travel companion.

- Twelve months is the usual limit on a round-the-world ticket. If you want to stay longer it may still be best to forfeit the final part and buy an extra flight home.

- Prices – bargain tickets start at around £800 plus taxes but are more typically £1,000–£2,000

- Flight itineraries centre on major hubs. Consider your time and method of moving out from the cities to more interesting areas.

The purchase of my own ticket took about a month. When my 85-day flight itinerary is finally confirmed it sounds incredible, with its promise of exotic spice ports and breathtaking landscapes:

Manchester – Amsterdam (transit) – Nairobi, Kenya – Dar Es Salaam, Tanzania – Dubai (transit) – Cochin, India – Sri Lanka (transit) – Kuala Lumpur (transit) – Denpasar, Bali – Kuala Lumpur (transit) – Sri Lanka – Singapore (transit) – Auckland, New Zealand – Fiji (transit) – Honolulu – New York (transit) – Manchester

I notice that the ticket is a Worldwide Traveller and cost the competition sponsor a hefty £2,560 – a price that partly relates to the number of miles I'm travelling and also the time of year. By choosing the Christmas period I've unwittingly selected the most expensive time to travel. Despite booking as early as June, it has been a struggle to get a flight into Auckland close to Christmas Day. Cheaper times are usually February to June (excluding Easter).

My second surprise is that I need yet more flights. More flights? I already seem to be spending enough time in Asian airports to write a guide to duty-free shopping. The trouble is that even with this ticket I'm not actually reaching many of my destinations. My safari in Kenya strands me in Zanzibar, a long way from my next flight out of Dar Es Salaam. Next, Bali is the closest I can get on a world ticket to Java, so I'm left pondering domestic Indonesian airlines and ferries. And lastly, some research into Honolulu's Polynesian cocktail culture quickly persuades me I need to hop onto some of the less-commercialised islands of Hawaii. And how can I do that? I groan to discover there's no ferry system, just more flights.

At the final reckoning I count 25 flights on my itinerary. This includes another nine short domestic flights I buy myself at a cost of around £350. One thing I'm discovering about my Monster Itinerary is that I don't actually seem to have a lot of time left to travel from place to place. So despite good eco-intentions, flying across that gulf or desert is just so much more convenient than the alternative land arrangements.

LAURA'S TIPS: Airtime comfort

✓ If you live outside London, ask for a connection from your local airport. It will probably be cheap and a blessing on your final leg home.

✓ Comfort and health are much higher priorities for older travellers. For the lowdown on comfort see www.airlinequality.com and for safety records check out www.airsafe.com.

✓ Sleeping on an airport bench is horrible and a security risk. For long airport stopovers book in at airport hotels or air transit rooms in advance.

✓ Avoid stress by using exclusive airport lounges. See www.holidayextras.co.uk to book lounges or join www.prioritypass.com for access to 500 VIP lounges in more than 90 countries.

✓ Business and first class can be very different concepts to different airlines. Ask about fully reclining seats, legroom and privacy before splashing out on what may only be larger seats and free alcohol.

Carbon emission

It is impossible not to be aware of the growing moral force in travel, variously called eco-travel, responsible tourism, green holidays or sustainable tourism. My simple interpretation of this tangled controversy is that as travellers, we must do our utmost not to unwittingly destroy the unique cultures and landscapes we travel to. Yet by flying so far and so often, carbon emissions are insidiously affecting our planet. On the other hand, by travelling to countries such as Kenya with nature reserves created and sustained by tourism, there have to be benefits to the local people. And I have always believed that contact between different peoples, however contrived it may appear, is basically a good thing that results in greater tolerance and understanding. This is a controversial area and one I can't ignore as I travel. Just 10 of the world's richest countries account for nearly 60% of all international travel. The last thing an enlightened traveller wants to do is damage the unique cultures they have come to see.

Sea travel

My mother used to tell me of her long voyage home to Holland every two years from Sumatra via the Suez Canal to the south of France. It took months but it sounded like the perfect way to travel, gliding past a slow cavalcade of exotic vistas. Today's equivalent is the cruise ship with its many advantages over aircraft: slow pace and genuine sense of distance travelled, luxury surroundings and scarcely a chance to lift a suitcase. The bonuses for older and less-fit passengers are also the absence of stressful overnight stops in strange hotels and early morning starts. However, big cruise ships are criticised as serious polluters, although a new breed of eco-friendly cruise lines is slowly emerging. Another complaint is the distance that the floating hotel puts between its guests and the countries visited. Charles and Elize overcame this by combining the first three-week leg of P&O's four-month round the world cruise from Southampton to Mumbai followed by a 10-week luxury tour of India:

'We knew a luxury cruise would be a vivid contrast to travelling overland in India. It was wonderful to sail across the Mediterranean and through the Suez Canal to reach India. We left at the beginning of January and it was still cool in Europe so our acclimatisation was gradual. Surprisingly, although we are in our 50s we were relative youngsters on board the ship. The pace appealed but after three weeks we were keen to start our travels around India. I loved only having to unpack once, and whenever you came back from trips it was like returning to your own home. We would love to go back to certain places like Luxor or Cairo to explore them in more depth.'

An alternative to unstinting luxury is the cargo ship voyage. The time spent staring out at sea will be far greater than on a cruise ship, although your cabin may be larger. Groups of passengers are usually small: around 12–16 people. Surprisingly, once long waits in ports and the extra costs of a single supplement are taken into account, cargo ships are not much cheaper than cruises. A round-the-world trip by cargo ship costs around £6,500 and lasts 84 days. Operators include www.strandtravel.co.uk and www.cruisepeople.co.uk.

Alternatively, you may be sufficiently skilled to sail yourself across the ocean. For many boat lovers it's a lifetime's dream to sail around the Greek islands or the Caribbean. There are strict seasons for these areas (May to October for Greece and October to May for the Caribbean) and seasonal routes further afield should you want to circumnavigate the globe. Clearly, level of fitness, lots of experience and a sense of adventure are paramount, as is your skill level in fields from skipper training to first aid. Check out specialist organisations like the Royal Yachting Association for advice and training (www.rya.org.uk).

Ron, 72, has sailed for many years, mooring his boat in Greece from where he explores the Greek Islands for a few months each summer. He offers a warning to any casual sailors:

LAURA'S TIPS: Reducing the damage

It's unavoidably true that the most damage you will do is via carbon emissions:

✓ Using the train, cycling or public transport are the best options. Check your carbon footprint and consider an offset at either www.climatecare.org or www.carbonneutral.com.

✓ Newer airlines are not only more comfortable but also less polluting. www.airfleets.net has details.

✓ Some commentators argue that on balance it's beneficial to fly to countries that need your tourist money and spend cash locally.

✓ Taking a gap year rather than short holidays is a perfect example of the Rough Guide's positive new policy, 'Fly Less, Stay Longer'.

✓ For more information about travelling responsibly get yourself a copy of **The Green Travel Guide** (Paul Jenner and Christine Smith, Crimson Publishing 2008)

'With sailing, you're on your own. If the engine fails or there's bad weather or an accident, you need to sort it out yourself. One day a piece of plastic sheeting wrapped around the rudder. I got down in the dinghy and had to lean right out under the boat with a carving knife to free it. It was very cold and I couldn't free it at *first. I lost all feeling in my hands and then I had a terrible thought. I realised I might be carving through my own arm. I shot up and was so relieved to see my arm was only slightly cut. People are used to having a phone and ringing a repairman. On the boat there's just you and the elements. That's the amazing thing about it when things are going well. But it's just you and the elements when things go wrong, too.'*

Rail travel

The romance of a long train journey can often be the inspiration for a truly great journey. The Trans-Siberian railway, South Africa's Blue Train or Japan's bullet trains conjure visions of adventure travel with all the comforts and no sacrifice of magnificent views from your window. You can now buy excellent value InterRail passes at any age for travel in up to 30 participating European countries. Good options include a flexi-pass that offers 10 days' rail travel within 22 days (currently under £300), or for more comfort buy an unlimited first-class pass giving a month's rail travel covering all 30 countries (currently around £600). For advice on best rail pass options and also inspiring train tours from The Orient Express to PeruRail, one of the highest rail routes on earth, see www.seat61.com or www.internationalrail.com.

Abby, 42, had just split up with her partner when she decided to visit eastern Europe with a friend:

'I wanted to see how eastern Europe had changed since the fall of communism. The fact that these countries had been isolated and oppressed interested me. I bought a rail pass and then added on extra journeys which didn't cost much as the fares are so low. It's also an eco- and people-friendly way to travel. I really enjoyed my train journeys. Sometimes I would read, write my journal or just look out of the window. There was always someone interesting to chat to.'

Ajay describes himself as 'no rail fanatic' but trains were part of the reason he travelled to Burma:

> 'The reason for travelling by train is to see everything at ground level. Flying deprives us of this opportunity. I particularly wanted to see the Gothiek rail viaduct, spanning two mountains. I learnt about it from Paul Theroux's book The Great Railway Bazaar (Penguin 1995). It was an exhilarating experience to traverse it in the engine of the train, getting a bird's eye view (my guide's uncle was driver that day so that's how I got to sit in the engine).'

Train travel in developing countries is not always a luxury experience. While backpacking Kate and Keith also found the trains in Thailand didn't quite fit their expectations:

> 'We decided to take the night train from Bangkok to Chiang Mai. I had this romantic notion of being lulled to sleep by the sound of the train on the tracks. Well, sleep was the last thing that happened. It was like lying down in a rickety no-suspension freight train.'

George experienced the sense of claustrophobia of a long train journey when he fulfilled an ambition to cross Australia on the Indian Pacific train:

> 'Climbing into the silver carriages in Perth, my heart leapt when I discovered the economy carriages were only half full. But soon I felt a bit rough and over the next few hours developed full-blown flu. The windows started heating up with the fierce sun but thankfully I kept drifting off into delirium. By morning and arrival in Cooke I had the rasping voice of Darth Vader and was getting through toilet rolls every half-hour with my tap-like nose. I survived the day chatting to the oddballs on the train but next morning woke at 4am with a sore throat and realisation that everyone around me was also sniffing and coughing. By Monday

I was reduced to wandering around looking for a space and found a bit of room on the floor behind some seats and curled up but couldn't get comfortable. By the time I got to Sydney at 11am, after three delirious days, all I could do was stagger off to find a hostel and sleep, totally relieved to have got off that tin can of circulating bacteria.'

Travelling overland

There comes a time on every trip when it is important to slow down to the local pace. Overland travel comes in as many varieties as there are forms of transport: walking, cycling, driving, taking local transport or a tour bus. Most travellers opt for a variety of transport to change the pace and the view as they travel.

At 54, Tim sold his business and his boat and decided to take the trip he had promised himself for years. Taking his own caravan, his plan was basically to just drive and take time out to think about his life:

'I had no itinerary really, just a drive straight down to Agadir in Morocco with my caravan and then use that as a base to visit Marrakesh, Essaouira, Tan Tan, Guelmim and the Sahara and the Atlas Mountains. I had no plans, just sort of went with the flow. Everything was fine apart from me forgetting some stuff, like Green Card insurance (not required for Europe, but it is for Morocco), and not having enough money!'

Polly, a volunteer worker in South Africa, chose to take public transport to explore the country on her own:

'I decided to head north for a while. Instead of taking the easy option of flying the vast distance I travelled by bus. I spent weeks on dusty roads travelling the Eastern Cape, through the Transkei and up through Zululand and finally coming to rest in Swaziland.

I don't mind admitting it was hard going; at times the bus was up to five hours late, making my arrival times at my next rest point in the early hours of the morning. Consequently I was too late and too tired to find a meal. It was an amazing journey though and well worth the effort.'

While working for a charity in Africa, Emrys also travelled overland and has advice for those attempting similar journeys:

'Don't give yourself too many time constraints. Be prepared to change your itinerary. Always have a book or a radio because if you're travelling by public transport it can break down and you wait for ever. It's a good idea to go to some of the rest houses frequented by travellers because they are bang up-to-date with what's going on.'

Joanne and George are a mother and son who set off backpacking to explore Australia together. Sticking together for three months, they didn't have a strict itinerary and decided where to go week by week:

'We did the east coast of Australia using tour buses like the Oz Experience that pre-package a few sights and "experiences" like turtle-watching and some ghastly sheep-shearing. The best bits were when we were more independent. Hiring a jeep to drive up to Cooktown in the far north was a huge laugh and also scary when the roads flooded, we were attacked by giant insects, and George lost the car keys in some spooky abandoned Maori caves – thankfully they turned up in the ignition so we just had to break into the car!'

Linda and James also got a rest from their backpacks after reaching Australia and hired a campervan for six weeks. The freedom of the dusty road transported them to some wonderful wildlife – as long as the tyres stayed inflated:

'First stop was Pinnacles National Park and a stunning sunset after seeing dingos, kangaroos and ostrich. Next, we were lucky enough to be in the sea when the wild dolphins swam in. One was so close we could have touched it. Incredible.

'We had a bad start next day when we woke up to a flat tyre. It's your worst nightmare to find the spare also flat, the place is full of flies – they just want to get in your ears and up your nose – and the mobile has no signal. Approximately one car passes an hour. Luckily, one passed with a couple of lovely ladies from Manchester so James hopped in and went for help. Almost four hours later our mechanic arrived to find me sweltering inside the van with a towel over my head to keep the flies away, pumped up the spare and we were back on the road. An experience – but not one we hope to repeat.'

Much overland travel is likely to be in the back of a minibus on a tour. Josh was just one traveller who found overland across Asia hard going. Eking out his savings for a year by following the backpacker trail, he also recalls some legs of the journey as 'a bizarre mix of highs and lows':

'I took the cheapest available tour from Thailand to Cambodia. The scenes after the border crossing were amazing. Huts lined the road full of half-naked families basking in hammocks surrounded by smoke, tending fires or congregating in little groups watching our battered minivan bounce along. When I say bounce, did we rock and roll. I've never ever encountered such a bad road. We're talking potholes that could swallow a shopping trolley. Nevertheless we made it and our minibus finished at an adequate guesthouse where I took a room at a great price ($3) per night.'

The Asian minibus experience also eventually got to Kate and Keith as they traversed Asia:

'We were going to try crossing overland to Cambodia but heard loads about the nightmare bus journeys people have had so decided to fly. Keith and I refuse to get in any more minibus. All I can say is that the Thais really take this reincarnation thing seriously: they regularly overtake other vehicles on blind bends – no problem.'

So, to cover the big distances, most travellers opt for air travel. It's fast, relatively safe and should be reliable. Or so it says on the ticket. But meanwhile, in Amsterdam, I'm finding that what is says on the ticket isn't necessarily what you get.

Day 1 Amsterdam, The Netherlands 8.30am

Flight number one (of my total of 25) has just landed. I'm in Amsterdam but it is mayhem here at 8.30am on a Monday morning. I can't wait to get on my next flight and take a long, lazy nap. Only there's a very big problem. When I try to check in, the blonde ice maiden flicks a few computer keys and says, 'I am afraid this flight to Nairobi is overbooked. You have no seat.' I clutch the counter feeling woozy, like someone hearing very tragic news very suddenly. 'But I've got a confirmed ticket,' I wail, shoving it towards her. 'How can there be no seat? It was booked in June for goodness sake! This is outrageous.' But all I get is a robotic reply. 'Every airline overbooks seats. Go to the gate and maybe they can sort something out. It is no problem anyway. You can fly back to London and try to get another flight.' I can what? No problem? To do a U-turn on my first leg and hang around Heathrow all day trying to cadge a lift to Africa? A vague condition of my safari trip surfaces in my mind. Something about if you miss the first meeting, you have to catch up with the others on your own and at your own expense. Just what I need. A wild goose chase through the African bush.

'Why me?' I demand.

'A computer chose you,' robot woman replies. Why, thank you very much, Mr Random Chip.

An hour later I'm in a queue at the gate after my seventh nerve-propelled trip to the toilet of the day. I am genuinely astounded that half of the population of Amsterdam appears to want to cram themselves on this plane while half the population of Nairobi appears to be returning home with giant packages. During an energetic rugby scrum I at last glimpse The Final Desk where I'm going to have to make my appeal for a seat. A worrying number of other people with anxious faces appear to be hanging around it too. I may be very tired, upset and on the verge of adult incontinence but with my last shred of sense I realise I need a strategy to persuade the Desk Person to give me a seat. I think back to all those airline documentaries on television where people rant and explode at the airline staff and generally entertain the public with enjoyable armchair *schadenfreude*. Oh, what fools they look, we chortle. And fancy not having a proper ticket. Ho, ho.

I recall a snippet from my business psychology days: 'It is very difficult for people to refuse a direct appeal for help.' So that's what I do. When I finally reach the head of the queue the woman looks just as robotically blonde and efficient as the last one.

'Can you please help me? I need a seat on this plane,' I explain.

I get the standard answer. The flight is overbooked, I have to wait but they will fly me back to London. I try again.

'Can you please help me,' I repeat in quiet desperation. 'I'm travelling alone. I need to be in Nairobi for a meeting. If I miss the meeting I won't be able to meet the rest of the group. I have people waiting for me at the airport. Please can you help me?'

The woman doesn't even look at me again, just flicks a few more keys and thrusts something in my hand. 'It's up at the front,' is all she says, and turns away.

It's a boarding pass. I truly don't care where it is – in the hold or even in one of those gigantic cases. But when I get on board I'm directed to a huge reclining seat in the front and handed a glass of champagne. Hooray! I've been upgraded to business class. Beside me is the permanent secretary to the Kenyan government, a charming chap who teaches me snippets of Swahili and tells me all about his family home up-country. I'm so relieved I lift my champagne flute and toast that lady on the desk. Her unexpected act of kindness has given me quite a boost but frankly, my nerves could have done without the extra adrenal shots. It may have cost a small fortune but just how secure is this ticket of mine?

THE FINAL COUNTDOWN

Day 1 Over the Sahara 6pm

Night is falling across the African plain as our aircraft speeds towards Nairobi. My new friend, the Kenyan permanent secretary, has had his fill of whisky and has reclined his seat to fall fast asleep beside me. I'm exhausted but too excited to sleep. The view through the window is beautiful, empty and unsettling; a darkling nothingness without towns or houses. There's a strange new emptiness in my life too, that allows me to absorb all these new sights and feelings. It's the death of my To Do list. Love them or hate them, a grown-up gap year needs plenty of pre-planning and the simplest way to keep track of everything is to list it and tick it off. All too soon it becomes a monster, dominating every waking moment. It's largely living as a slave to that giant To Do list that has driven me into my pre-departure stress-out. Here's what my own journal was obsessing over one month before departure:

Countdown — one month to go

With only one month to go each day seems to be passing in a flash as I struggle to be ready in time to leave. Despite what feels like months of hard labour preparing myself, my list never seems to get shorter: it runs from currency exchange to hotel bookings, health check-up, bank transfers and the creation of files of information to take with me.

None of this betrays the emotional upheaval beneath all my surface dithering. I just can't decide if I'm going off on some wonderful creative odyssey or a lonely, nerve-shattering nightmare. In the middle of the night when I can't sleep, the nightmare option always wins – at best a vision of me being lonely and miserable and, at worst, of me being ill, bombed to bits or just plain dead. The news doesn't help. There are appalling mudslides in Java, quite close to Surabaya, my airport of departure. Nor is the news from Sri Lanka good as the civil war appears to be straying into the area I will be visiting.

Even deeper than this there is plain old guilt. About leaving my husband to fend for himself. About leaving my father-in-law who is struggling in hospital after a heart attack. And worst of all, about leaving my mother who has serious health problems, especially for the three weeks when my sisters and I (all my mother's family in fact) will be meeting up to achieve our long-cherished goal of exploring Indonesia together.

Leaving your life behind

As an older gap traveller it is far more difficult to extract yourself successfully from your life at home than it is for a university-age gapper. Of course you can just leap onto a plane on a mid-life whim but the chances are that if you have reached anything like a mature age, this is not a great idea. A host of nasty penalties from bureaucracies with nothing better to do may suddenly fall down on your head. So, as far ahead as six months before take-off, it pays to start planning. There may be employment to finish, finances to tie up and your home and car to make arrangement for.

Finishing work

Many grown-up gappers choose to take a long trip to celebrate freedom from decades of work. It may be retirement or redundancy, but however work ends, any lump sum you receive needs to work hard to produce investment income for you while you are away. Redundancies, like so much in life, can also often involve slippage, as computer worker Elize, 55, found out before her extended honeymoon to India:

> 'We were actually going to travel a year earlier as I had volunteered for redundancy after the business was relocated to Uruguay. But at the 11th hour they asked me to stay on for another 12 months. It was flattering I suppose and as I didn't want to take my pension yet, I agreed. It actually turned out to be a bad idea as I had to work incredibly hard and took a placement in Moscow that proved to be a bit of a disaster.'

Career break

Taking a career break from work is an increasingly common benefit for those who want to keep their job open. After all, your career often represents a major asset in terms of years invested and skills developed. Even if you have come to the end of your tether with your job, you may feel different after a year's refreshment and be grateful for a resumption of regular pay cheques.

Your case for a career break will be helped by putting your case for the benefits of a break, for example development of leadership skills, confidence-building or useful language skills. Another strategy is to try to create an attractive link from your trip back to your employer, such as a spell learning valued new skills or making international contacts. Make your boss' life easy by packaging the whole idea including suggestions for who will do your job and how you will seamlessly hand over work.

THE FACTS: Career break policies

- Usually you will need to have worked for two years before being eligible.

- Terms vary about return to your current job or an equivalent job, and also whether the break will be paid or, more usually, unpaid.

- Find out if anyone has gone before you and what precedents exist.

- Consider timing: your boss will be more likely to let you go at a slack time. And from your own point of view, get any pay reviews, bonuses or increments in the bag before you leave.

- Double-check arrangements for your pension, and also whether you will break your continuous service record (important for many rights such as redundancy pay and pension).

- Get it all in writing.

- And if you have to resign to get away: say goodbye on friendly terms. You will need a reference on return and a surprising number of career gappers do go back to their old company.

Resigning from work

For eight out of 10 career breakers, the pull to travel is too irresistible to get into long negotiations – they simply resign. When Joanne decided to fly out to Australia, her eldest son George surprised her by suggesting he would resign and come along too. At 29 he was able to apply for an Australian Working Holiday Visa, available to young people aged 18–30 for 12 months (www.immi.gov.au). This scheme allows a stay of 12 months and up to six months' work with each employer:

'I had worked non-stop since graduation and I needed a change. My friends and people in general looked fairly unhappy and stressed. I realised that I didn't want to follow that path and wanted to look at other options. A working holiday appealed as the only way to stay out for a full year.'

Another career breaker, Paul, also viewed his lifestyle as something to escape from before it was too late:

'The key driver was that I was working in the UK looking towards what I would call a bleak future in terms of achieving a life goal, with houses and lifestyle being so expensive. I could see my future ending up as working long hours, living in a small townhouse in a large city with depressing weather and calling that a "success" in relation to other people. I believe that success and happiness should hold no boundaries and in the UK boundaries are all too obvious.'

Tim, 54, was also looking for a total escape from all the constraints of home. He describes himself as:

'Separated/single, no money, children grown up, no ties, sold my business for less than I owe, and went off to Morocco with a caravan. No mid-life crisis, just a sort of crossroads that seems more like Spaghetti Junction.'

But for some travellers the decision is simple. When James and Linda set off around the world for seven months everything was refreshingly straightforward:

'We both love travelling – and hate work!'

Money matters

Tedious though it may sound, sorting out your finances in advance of departure is crucial. For a worry-free trip take time to overhaul your finances and de-clutter your life before you go.

Home finances checklist

- Pay off any loans before you go, or at least have direct debits set up to prevent any default problems.

- Cancel subscriptions to magazines, clubs, gyms or any other items you can save money on.

- Set up direct debits or standing orders to cover regular payments for insurance, council tax, utilities and any other regular outgoings. Consider a flexible payments mortgage.

- Check your house insurance policy for cover if the house is left empty. You may need a specialist insurer.

- Complete your tax return well in advance. If timing means you need to complete it while away, you will need a secure password from your tax office. Check out www.inlandrevenue.gov.uk.

- Travellers who cease employment often get a tax rebate. Apply to the tax office to have any refund paid directly into your bank account.

- If you will be away for more than a year, you may want to make voluntary national insurance payments. Contact www.hmrc.gov.uk.

- Tell your bank and credit card company where and for how long you intend to travel. Irregular spending patterns can trigger a distressing stop on your funds.

- And finally, do keep some savings for when you get back!

It makes good sense to have easy access to your money while away. The easiest methods are to set up both online banking and phone banking before you leave. Practise using both of these if you aren't familiar with them and be sure to learn (or store in a secure place) any passwords or codes. Be careful, however, when accessing your bank details in an internet café. Make sure the software isn't saving your passwords and log off and clear 'history' after using the computer. Phone banking is generally a safer option, but for this you will need to take your bank's international telephone number and remember that 0800 numbers are going to be useless.

If your affairs are complicated you may want to leave your finances in the care of someone you trust. The safest way to do this is to set up a special account with limited funds and have your friend or relative sign a third party mandate that allows them access only to those limited funds. If, however, you have some large unfinished business such as a house sale to finalise, you may need to appoint a power of attorney. This is not normally necessary for day-to-day affairs and should only be given to someone you completely trust not to help themselves to all your worldly fortune.

If travelling for a long period to one part of the world, it makes sense to be able to use a local bank. Before flying out to Ghana for two years' charity work Emrys considered how he could access the small stipend the charity would pay him:

> 'I did open a bank account with a large multinational bank because I knew there was a branch in the capital of Ghana and it would be fairly secure. That way you aren't liable to foreign currency fluctuations and if it's with a multinational bank you are fairly secure.'

However much care you take to tie up your financial affairs, something can nevertheless always strike out of the blue. Josh painstakingly paid off all his debts before leaving the UK but by taking a cheap room in his final weeks of pre-travel saving, he opened himself up to an unexpected risk:

'While I was in southern Asia my friend was getting my redirected mail including a series of demands for a debt I'd never heard of. I tracked it down to my last cheapo flat in London where my mail was left in the hall and no doubt one of my neighbours availed themselves of my bank details and ordered a load of stuff. Pretty soon there were heavy legal letters from debt collectors. Thankfully my friend chased it up and eventually proved I'd not ordered the stuff. It took a few long distance phone calls to sort out and a letter signed by me saying I wanted my friend to act on my behalf. Without her it could easily have escalated to a court appearance and all sorts of nasty consequences.'

Your home

For many mature travellers their home represents their most significant money-making resource. It is tempting to imagine big rental money rolling in to fund your trip. However, in practice many travellers opt for the security of letting someone they know stay in their house rather than risking a more lucrative agreement with strangers. Linda and James' experience is typical in terms of the types of obstacles set in the way of short-term landlords:

'We rented out the house. Our original plan was to do this via a letting agency but in the end they needed certain safety checks and also to notify the mortgage company and the insurance company and none of these seemed very helpful. Because we went in December there were few people looking to rent (especially for only six months) so the letting agency wanted us to leave the keys, but we wanted to know who the tenant was going to be. At the last minute someone I worked with decided to stay at the house. It meant we could leave some of the big furniture (we stored the rest in a family garage) so we had a very informal agreement. Nothing was put in writing, they paid rent into our bank each month, and all our direct debits came out as usual, including mortgage and

insurance. The only thing they changed was the council tax. We had to go slightly under our costs to get them to agree so made a loss rather than a profit for the rental.'

Other travellers, like Fran, 70, preferred to leave their homes empty with keys entrusted to friends and family in case of an emergency:

'I switched everything off after having a flood when I came back from Spain on another holiday. I gave out a key to my next-door neighbour, son and a friend who was coming in to look after the house plants. I didn't do anything about the mail. I pay everything by direct debit. I also applied for a credit card so I'd have a spare and arranged to pay it off every month out of my bank. I let the credit card people know where I was going and that was about it.'

Also fearful of floods while locking up her remote cottage for the winter, Joanne took extra care against bad weather:

'My stone cottage was at the edge of open country and prone to electricity cuts. I emptied the freezer and switched off everything like computers in case of a surge. I was worried the temperature might fall below freezing so I set the gas heating to come on very low every night so the pipes wouldn't burst. I also set lamps to come on automatically in the evening and left keys and emergency contact details with family and neighbours.'

Naturally the way to make the most money from your home is to sell it. This option is less appealing to older travellers unless they are 'between houses' or intending to move abroad permanently. The disadvantages of buying or renting again on return to the UK are usually too daunting. Younger gappers, however, are more likely to view property as a means to fund long-term travel. Kate and James sold not one but two houses before setting off for two years' travel:

'Well, it finally happened – both houses were sold (our parents' house had been on the market for nearly three years so it was a big moment). My parents are now dead by the way – we are not fleecing them and then running off. You have to have a sense of humour about these things! We were also on our fourth prospective buyer for our house – so an even bigger moment. The advantage of having a mid-life crisis gap year is that you have a lot more cash to blow.'

Your car

Unless you are driving to your destination, you need to make arrangements for your car. Leaving it out on the drive through the winter will be both a temptation to thieves and vandals and a rapid way of hurrying its depreciation. Basically, you can lend it, store it or sell it.

Leaving your car in the garage isn't ideal as it should be run at least weekly. It may be easier and cheaper to lend your car to a family member or friend so that it gets regular runs and attention. Don't forget to insure the new driver and leave details of your breakdown and servicing agents. Professional storage is expensive at around £70 per month but that should include regular driving and professional cleaning. You will need to complete a SORN (Statutory Off Road Notice) for the DVLA and also tell your insurer.

If you will be away for six months or longer it makes sense to sell your car. You will have more money for the trip and none of the expense or worry of maintaining the car at home. Selling a car is another of those open-ended tasks that tends to take longer than you expect, so start early. Selling to a dealer will generally be quicker than a private sale and also safer in terms of your own safety and the validity of a cheque. If you do sell privately, insist on a banker's draft rather than a personal cheque – the last thing you need in the run-up to leaving is difficulties with a bouncing cheque.

When mother and son Joanne and George set off for Australia they took different approaches to dealing with their cars. George sold his, as he needed the cash:

> 'I started trying to sell my Peugeot a month or so before I left by placing ads on the internet. But as time ticked by without a taker I got desperate. The tax was running out and I needed to get rid of it quickly. In the end I took it to a dealer and took what he offered. It was less than I wanted but it was cash that I could use to buy traveller's cheques the same day.'

His mother Joanne couldn't bear to get rid of her car and stored it in her mother's garage for the winter:

> 'I didn't think very hard about it as I loved my car. I just declared SORN and locked it up. But when I got back it was as dead as a doornail and needed a new battery and a whole series of expensive repairs. Finally, I couldn't afford to run it and I set out to sell it. The penny dropped that if I'd sold it before I set off I'd not only have had extra money but would have avoided all the repair costs and a winter's depreciation.'

Leaving emotional baggage

It may be possible to put a subscription on hold or a car in storage, but when it comes to personal relationships there are no neat ends. It may be your children who hear your plans unfold in horror or your partner whose work means they can't travel with you. Or your beloved cat who needs a home. Or it may be that, like me, you have an elderly dependent who needs just as much daily care as a child to keep them safe.

For those friends and family who are simply worried for you, or even hostile to the idea of a big trip, the best response is to offer to keep in touch. Chapter Seven covers ways to communicate with those back home but, needless to say, frequent updates on your safety and whereabouts should do much to calm the concerns of those left at home.

Of course the joke about Spending your Kids' Inheritance really could mean that your children feel you are having a good time at the expense of their future legacies. Consequently you feel guilty. But why should you? As luxury honeymooner and financial adviser Charles says:

> *'One danger of preserving your estate for your children is that the adage "Fly business class – or your children will," may just come true!'*

Care for dependents

If you are the main carer for someone, you will need to arrange alternative care. Do check out all the options well in advance, from private agencies to local networks of friends and voluntary groups. Local social services should be able to help you with respite or care at home, but these can take an age to sort out. It can take endless patience to find the right care but so long as the dependent is safe and secure, whether in a nursing home or with family or friends, don't allow yourself to fall too deeply into a miasma of guilt. For many carers this is their once-in-a-lifetime chance to do something they want to do. Take it and enjoy it.

Leaving your partner

Leaving a partner behind can be especially troubling but common sense tells us that a relationship worth having will survive a temporary separation. No loving partner would want to deny a spouse their moment of freedom after a lifetime of nine-to-five or decades of childcare. When Sue retired she simply wasn't prepared to wait for her husband to travel with her:

> 'My husband was not too happy and asked if I couldn't put it off for five years so that he could come too when he retires. But I felt it was something I had to do after bringing up three children and working. It was sort of a treat to myself.'

Joanne had just started a relationship when she set off with her son George. Three months earlier she had met a man who she was convinced was her soulmate:

> 'It was a dreadful wrench leaving Mark as we were very much in the throes of falling in love. But everything was already planned before I met him and I would never have let George down. Or myself – I wanted to celebrate being alive after being ill, and travelling was the perfect expression of my new positive attitude. I did have the odd little weep, though, and some expensive long distance phone calls. Nevertheless I thought it was a good test of our love and if it was real I knew we'd survive as a couple.'

Countdown — one week to go

I've had a terrible week. My father-in-law is due to come home from hospital in the next few days and I feel just wretched that I won't be around to support him. He's 90 now, and I fear the worst. My husband Laurence, on top of his heavy teaching load, has to deal with arranging his social services care, organising meals and a care alarm and all the other paraphernalia needed to keep a very frail old person at home. Then, this morning, Galle in Sri Lanka was on the news where two sailors have been killed and 26 wounded in a suicide bomb attack. I'm going to be staying in Galle on my own in December. I must be mad.

However, I have had one brainwave. After ringing endless care agencies I have decided to pay my friend Yvonne, who has professional caring skills, to live in with my mum while we're all away. I've also decided to lend Yvonne my car so she and my mum can motor around together and the engine will get a good run through the winter. With time running out I'm having to delegate my last few travel arrangements. In preparation for our family meet-up in Indonesia my sister is booking hotels, and my son is making all my ferry arrangements in New Zealand. But one thing I can't delegate is packing. The blue bag on wheels is looking decidedly petite beside the huge heap of clothes piled up in the spare bedroom. I've been putting it off but I can't avoid it – it's time to start packing.

KNAPSACK NIGHTMARE

Countdown — 24 hours to go

I've been hit by unscheduled activities all day. The worst moment came when I discovered a whole series of urgent assessments a college has forgotten to send me. They could have been completed months ago and now I'll either have to pick them up by email on the road or leave them until I return. Then there are the nice but time-consuming bits to the day. People have been ringing me all day to wish me bon voyage. It's lovely, but has set me back hours. And the small bits take time – like posting off advance birthday cards and writing out paying-in slips for my husband to post cheques to the bank. By the time I start ironing I'm shattered. Then there's a sudden crisis when my spare contact lenses aren't where I put them. When I finally start to pack I find that within a few minutes my bag looks scarily full – but the pile of clothes isn't getting much smaller.

Clothes

I've had to develop a few rules about clothes to help me reduce my wardrobe – though obviously it's not quite reduced enough yet:

1   Keep to a few dirt-deflecting colours. I've gone for khaki and blue after learning that white is a real problem in any country with dust.

2   Bring clothes combinations that cover arms, legs and head if travelling to culturally sensitive areas.

3   Only take items that are very comfortable – even when wearing a thick money belt around your waist.

4   Only pack items that are easy to wash and drip dry.

5   Forget the evening wear and pack junk jewellery and sparkly flip-flops to jazz up your daywear at night.

In the end I take the following clothes:

1 fleece
8 summer tops
3 cover-up shirts
1 nightie
2 swimsuits
2 sarongs
4 pairs of trousers
1 long skirt
1 sundress
2 pairs of sandals
flip-flops
sun hat
sunglasses
underwear
socks
cheap jewellery
head scarf

LAURA'S TIPS: Choosing luggage

Wheels or no wheels — that is the question. The verdict is split between those who choose a backpack (usually younger) and those who swear by luggage they can roll along (us older folk). Other luggage issues to consider are:

✓ The bigger the bag the more you will take. Do yourself a favour and buy small.

✓ You should be able to lift your own bag with relative ease, for example onto a high bus platform or shelf.

✓ Buy for strength and durability. Your bag will be thrown and dropped regularly and needs to be built to last.

✓ Think about carrying your bag over long distances and how manoeuvrable it will be in a crowd. Can you run or climb stairs with your luggage?

✓ Check airline size and weight restrictions.

✓ Useful features of all bags are lots of zippered compartments and a few lockable pockets.

The capsule wardrobe

For both men and women the aim is to carry as few lightweight coordinating items as possible. A ratio of three or four 'bottoms' can be matched up with as many as eight 'tops', all to be washed in rotation. For a man the basic wardrobe would include:

> *1 fleece*
> *3 or 4 trousers and shorts*
> *mix of long and short sleeved tops*
> *1 rain jacket*
> *socks*
> *underwear*
> *sunhat*
> *trekking sandals*
> *flip-flops*
> *sunglasses*

Talking to other travellers, the insistent message is to travel light and take wheels. Paul is typical of those who packed for a year and then realised too late they took too much and in the wrong bag:

> *'I probably should have had a wheeled trolley, rather than two large carrying bags. They take no effort and free up your hands to do other things. I took about 20kg of baggage which included a 4kg laptop. I ended up throwing lots of clothes away. If I packed again I'd pack very little, perhaps about 15kg. Everything can be bought when needed and washing machines are everywhere.'*

Josh carried less after a process of rigorously questioning what to take:

> *'I took one large bag on wheels and one shoulder bag for day trips and flights. I always ask myself when packing clothes "do I really like them and can I imagine wearing them soon?" It was surprising how often clothes didn't make it into my bag. But I didn't*

completely escape the packing minefield – I brought far too many books that weren't read.'

When Sue and her two boys aged 11 and 12 set off around the world they all took backpacks but had an ingenious strategy for clothing:

'Clothing wasn't a problem as luckily both the boys and I could get away with wearing the same clothes. We took several pairs of zip-off trousers, shorts, T-shirts and sports socks that would fit all of us. I did draw the line at wearing their underpants and took my own knickers, bikini and bras, but other than that we swapped clothes throughout the journey. My rucksack was huge – almost as big as me – but the boys had relatively sensible-sized ones so we had to make considered judgements on what we could take. No teddy bears, just Les the lesbian lizard (a toy) as a good luck charm.'

For very long trips it makes sense to try a different approach: forget packing for the whole journey and treat your baggage as entirely flexible, discarding and replacing items as you travel. Michael's approach was to buy and replace items as he moved around:

'I travel very light and only take hand luggage if going to Third World countries. I buy things there; it saves carrying heavy bags and is good for the local economy when you leave. It's far better to give your clothes away, so for example I've left clothes with a family living under plastic.'

One popular tip is to try to travel only with hand luggage. However, the almost daily change of regulations about hand luggage means that it can be hard to predict what size of bag (if any) will be allowed on a series of flights with different airlines. New anti-terror rules can upset the best laid plans at a day's notice, as Fran found just before she flew off in 2006:

'I went just as that hoo-ha about liquids in hand luggage was happening. So I was suddenly reduced down to just 20kg and no

hand luggage. Suddenly everything had to go into my case includ-
ing my rucksack. I had a very small handbag and I had my cam-
era around my neck and I just got away with that. I had to leave
all sorts behind.'

Overpacking is a real temptation, but it's a mistake you will feel in
your aching back all the way through your trip. Linda confessed
she took far too much around the world:

'We overpacked, despite reading everything to the contrary, and
ended up taking a pack of cards and a pair of football socks
around the world, completely unused. I also ended up discarding
umpteen tops that were not needed, just to make space. We
replaced a few clothes, and had to purchase cold-weather clothing
for New Zealand.'

Temperature changes are the bane of those trying to pack eco-
nomically and are a powerful reason not to stray into too many
different climes. Gapper hotspot New Zealand is one destination
famed for its 'four seasons in one day' and therefore demanding
packing ingenuity. Gilly, 64, coped with this by anticipating the
difference between the warm North Island and chilly mountains
and glaciers of the South Island:

'We decided to pack two large cases: one for the North Island and
the other for the South Island. On advice I took clothes for all sea-
sons. This worked well as we had one or two cold and wet days.
We left one case in the boot of the car and changed over when we
reached the South Island.'

Fran also split her packing between two vacuum bags that reduced
the volume of clothes to their minimum:

'I had two zippered bags that you can press all the air out of so you
get a lot more in. I kept the lightweight things in one and the
warmer things in the other. Some days it was very hot and others
it was snowing.'

Splitting your baggage is also a smart response when moving through two completely different experiences. Charles and Elize found the dress demands of their cruise totally different from the overland tour of India. Fortunately, they discovered that the cruise ship would store their case on board until they returned to the UK:

> 'The good thing was that there was no limit on luggage on the cruise and the cruise company allows you to leave your suitcases on board (for a fee) to continue on the world cruise and be picked up on return. So I could leave four evening dresses and all our more formal wear on the ship and just pack light for India.'

On the other hand you can just post your excess baggage home. It really is easier and often cheaper than lugging it around a few continents as Fran found:

> 'My walking boots took a lot of space. So I sent them home in a box from Auckland along with heavy cardigans, jumpers and paper stuff I didn't need. It's cheaper doing that than paying excess baggage on a plane.'

Health and toiletries

Six weeks before departure I booked an appointment to check out vaccinations. The outcome: vaccinations to prevent Yellow Fever, Hepatitis A, Hepatitis B, Meningitis and Rabies, and a course of malaria tablets. It cost £251 for vaccinations and another £42 for 100 malaria tablets. This was way over my budget but as I quibbled, my nurse took a long hard look at me and said, 'There's not much point in going all that way and dying is there?' Even I can't argue with that.

My next priority is to hand over £156 for travel insurance. After hours of internet searching I find a 90-day policy offering £2 million medical cover and the rare inclusion of cover in case of terrorist incidents.

LAURA'S TIPS: Packing your main bag

✓ Roll rather than fold clothes to avoid creases.

✓ Put liquids inside plastic bags so all your clothes won't be ruined if there's a burst.

✓ Never put any valuables or essential documents in checked-in baggage.

✓ Couples can distribute baggage across two cases as a safeguard against one case going missing.

✓ If your trip calls for very different gear at different stages consider posting some of it home once it's been used.

✓ Leave space for souvenirs and new clothes.

I've spent a long time trying to reduce my toiletries list as I'm a woman who does like to wallow in her creams and potions, but in the end I take:

Sun screen and block – starter bottles only – replenish on the road
Travel alarm – for all those early starts
Tweezers, safety pins, scissors, nail clippers, penknife – remember to pack in main luggage to avoid confiscation
Conditioning shampoo – one bottle of all-in-one
All-in-one liquid soap – available from hiking shops to wash clothes, body and even fruit

Anti-bacterial soap in a box – more compact than shower gel
Plastic bags – always useful
Mini sewing kit – just needle and threads
Mosquito repellent – strong DEET mix
Body lotion – combines as aftersun and foot cream
Toothbrush and paste – pack a toothbrush cover too, to avoid
    bacteria
Universal sink plug – great for washing and essential for contact
    lens users
Photos – soft album of all my loved ones
Deodorant

For the ladies

Tampons and pads – one month's supply then replenish
Mirror and basic make-up – most guides say forget make-up so I
    assume must be written by very naïve young men
Cleansing wipes
Nail polish/remover pads/nail file/foot file – to keep bare feet pretty
Fake tan – to avoid that lardy legs look
Hairclips and bands – to keep hair up for swimming

For the gentlemen

Shaving gear

Medical kit

It is possible to buy ready-packed medical kits but I'm not convinced they are good value for money. All that lint and bandage
seems a strange thing to carry around the globe. Instead, I recommend taking all your usual tablets and creams plus a few extras to
cope with insects and small infections:

Eye infection drops – the bane of contact lens wearers
Diarrhoea tablets and rehydration salts – essential for
    tummy trouble

THE FACTS: Travel insurance

You may feel you need a long holiday after working through the insurance minefield, especially if you are over 70 or have a pre-existing medical condition:

■ Most standard policies cover only 30-day trips and many have upper age limits. Check out the adventure travel companies for longer trips.

■ The issue for older travellers is likely to be adequate cover in a medical emergency. Look for at least £5 million cover and repatriation to fly you home. Help the Aged recommends up to £10 million cover for elderly clients.

■ If you have a pre-existing medical condition, be honest and prepared for even more ringing around. As a general rule, avoiding the USA should reduce your premium.

■ If the premium is still too high, ask about paying more excess on the policy.

■ Keep an eye on cancellation cover as well. If you had to cancel a pre-booked trip would you get your money back?

■ Be aware that your travel insurance will be invalidated if you travel to any country the Foreign Office has advised against travelling to (see Travel Advice on www.fco.gov.uk).

■ There is evidence that premium prices vary hugely. Shop around, search the internet and don't be disheartened.

Nasal decongestant – to relieve sinus pressure when flying
Prescription drugs – order what you need plus some over
Malaria tablets – again, enough plus some over
Travel sickness tablets – for boats and all those winding roads
Antihistamine – for allergies, hayfever and bites

Painkillers – your usual brand
Bite-easing cream – to ease the itch and discomfort

Exceptionally, a long trip to very remote areas will require some medical extras. Emrys and his team of charity workers were kitted out on the assumption that many items would be unavailable:

> 'You should have seen the box of condoms we were given to take over. The family planning clinic worked on the assumption we would all have sex four times a week for three years! And we took lots of needles and syringes. The locals do re-use them so you've got to be careful.'

Travel essentials

Finally there are those items that you don't want to be parted from – ever. My daypack, like the main bag it fits onto, is annoyingly petite. As I start stuffing it full of flight essentials I wonder how it will stand up to months of heavy duty. I'm also taking a small handbag made of hardy nylon in a dirt-resistant brown colour with lots of inner pockets and zips. My carry-on luggage includes the following long-haul essentials:

Trip file – soft plastic folder containing my itinerary, excerpts from guide books, hotel vouchers, copies of prescriptions, copies of essential travel documents – all the info I need on my trip.
PDA (Personal Digital Assistant) – mini computer combining phone/word processor/mp3/email and texting facility
Keyboard – folding Bluetooth mini-keyboard
Book – just the one for me plus four books to give as gifts. I also carry eight weight-free audio books on storage cards to slot into the PDA.
Digital camera – plus five storage cards
Leads and chargers – for the camera and PDA
Electrical plug adapter – for every continent

LAURA'S TIPS: Lost luggage

It has been estimated that one million passengers each year are left without their luggage for up to two days. As many as 250,000 of these go missing for longer.

✓ Always carry essential documents like travel vouchers and tickets, visas and immunisation cards on your person.

✓ Keep irreplaceable personal items like your travel journal, camera and storage cards close to you at all times.

✓ Other hand luggage essentials include prescription drugs, toothbrush and paste, spare spectacles or contacts, fresh underwear and small toiletries like a razor, deodorant or sun lotion.

✓ If two of you are travelling, distribute items between both bags.

✓ Be vigilant when checking in. Make sure that the correct three-letter airport code is stuck on your luggage (eg NBO for Nairobi). Then make sure you get the bar code receipt for your luggage (usually stuck on the back of your tickets).

✓ If your luggage goes missing you will be asked the make and style of your bag. Do you know it?

Spare knickers – in event of delays
Spectacles, spare contact lenses and solutions
Earplugs, neck cushion and eye mask – I love my sleep and need
    these for flights, even if I do look like an alien when wearing
    all at once.
Flight socks – to prevent DVT and balloon feet
Notebook and pens
Purse – for small change
Basic make-up and moisturiser
In-flight toothbrush and paste
Hairbrush
Anti-bacterial handwash

Finally, there is my moneybelt and the most vital three items of all: tickets, passport and credit card. After lots of research I have decided to carry the majority of my spending as plastic cards. I'm reyling on the presence of cash machines and banks everywhere except the most remote islands. As a back-up I'm also taking some US dollars in cash and emergency US dollar traveller's cheques. That's it. I am hoping most hotels and food and transport can be charged to my credit cards.

The moneybelt itself is new to me. This beige article with all the glamour of a used surgical bandage is to be my must-have item for the next few months. I practise putting it on and find the elastic has a nasty habit of pinging open. It's too late now, but I need to entrust my truly precious items to this tiny security pouch.

My moneybelt contains:
2 credit cards
1 debit card
$1,000 cash
$1,000 American Express traveller's cheques
Passport

Vaccination record/certificate

Travel insurance details

Driving licence – even if not planning to drive this is a useful
  secondary photographic identity card.

E111 – the EEC health card. Just in case I collapse over Europe.

Flight tickets

Hotel voucher – for first night

Emergency data card – home-made list of phone numbers and
  health data such as blood group and medications

LAURA'S TIPS: Healthy flying

✓ Travel in comfortable all-seasons layers and wear
  worn-in shoes.

✓ DVT socks promote blood flow and help avoid
  elephant-sized feet. Pacing the aisle and chair
  exercises will also help.

✓ Drink plenty of water and avoid caffeine-rich tea,
  coffee and fizzy drinks.

✓ Don't eat everything put in front of you. To avoid
  bloating provide your own healthy snacks.

✓ On a noisy trip, earplugs or headphones can help you
  sink into sleep.

I'm all set now. I can lift my bags (just) and though I feel like a sherpa with my daypack on I think I can cope. Under my skirt my fat moneybelt looks a bit like a false pregnancy. I'm afraid glamour will just have to give way to brute practicality on this trip. But on the other hand it is good to know I've left a fair amount of stuff behind. I keep in mind the items that come up again and again in traveller's tales of what not to take.

What not to take

Boots and shoes – the general consensus is that you can get by with one pair of trekking sandals. Unless hiking in hard conditions forget the boots or hire them.

Books – photocopy sections or break pages. Buy, share or borrow when you arrive. Download novels or podcasts.

Culturally insensitive clothes – vests, shorts and skimpy clothes for either sex are not recommended in many countries and may offend.

Insensitive items – anything linked to drugs, pornography or material critical of the country you are visiting

Treasured items – leave any heirlooms at home

Sleeping bag and pillow – unless camping in the mountains it will be too hot and sheets will be provided with your night's shelter.

Laptop – unless you are doing paid work on the road it's too heavy and a magnet for thieves.

Jeans – too heavy, too hot and take an age to dry

Hairdryer – there's a giant free one called the sun

Packing tips from real travellers

'In the future it would be better for us to take two smaller bags each, to make lifting easier.' Gilly

'Buy a child's waterproof drawstring kitbag for all your toiletries – great for those dawn trips to the bathroom.' Alex

'Travelling = accumulation. When packing, always leave space in your bag enabling you to buy as you travel, without worry.' Josh

'We spent about two weeks refining our needs prior to travelling and only purchased a few items of camping equipment and several dozen books en route.' Sue

'Take a lot of single dollars for tipping.' Fran

'Travel with a smile and an open heart – and always have a sarong in your backpack.' Polly

'Take more than one credit or bank card, and the international phone number to report any mishaps.' Joanne

'For ladies, a metre square of cotton fabric is invaluable – as a skirt/wrap, as a makeshift sheet or picnic rug or many more uses.' James and Linda

'You will want local clothes from markets and a few souvenirs so leave room in your case. Why carry all your usual boring old stuff around the world?' George

ON THE TOUR

Day 1 Nairobi, Kenya

Everything runs to plan as I'm ushered through customs eager to reach the safe zone of my pre-booked hotel. After all, night has already fallen in Nairobi – a city so infamous for its crime rate that it's nicknamed Nai-robbery. My driver Jomo is grinning in Arrivals with my name held high on a sign and I'm soon outside in the warm, pitch-black night. From across the concourse the voices of a choir singing African harmonies swells in a beautiful, rhythmic song. I can't understand a word but I couldn't have had a better welcome to this vibrant continent.

'Who are they?' I ask Jomo, spotting a group of track-suited young men gathered in a cluster at the airport entrance. They are huge dreadlocked men and in their colourful tracksuits look like characters from some New York gangland movie. Only they are swaying in time to their song and grinning as they whoop and clap and sing their hearts out.

'Dey are welcoming one of dere tribe home. He is der winner of some big atletic victory. So de tribe welcomes him beck wid dis song.'

I love the way Jomo chats away as we zoom off into the neon constellation of Nairobi with the radio lilting out African guitar music and the night air thick with the scents of diesel and hibiscus. I'm just beginning to calm down when Jomo tells me some alarming news. Apparently Nairobi has been invaded by giant bats. 'Dere are bads with 4ft wings living in the city. Dey live in the trees. You see dem?' My goodness, I had thought it looked like a fairly ordinary city up to now. I look up in the trees but can't see them yet. And there was me thinking Jurassic Park was a story. Four-foot bats? My stomach heaves again. Am I really up to all this wildlife malarkey?

Then I see them. Giant storks, actually, living in the huge trees planted along the central boulevard. Giant birds, then. Glad we've cleared that one up. My hotel comes into view behind huge anti-tank cement blocks and two guarded checkpoints as the Israeli Embassy is just across the road. I've no objection to all the high security in this city with its history of tragic embassy bombings. Just time to roll into my clean, neat bed and sleep like a log until my two alarm clocks rouse me from a semi-coma.

Taking a tour

For the first two weeks of my trip I've joined an organised group tour. It is a major decision facing all gap travellers, whether to take the independent route and see the world at your whim or enjoy the security and companionship of a group experience. The independent route is my usual choice on holidays but this trip is different. The result is that it's the most expensive fortnight of my whole tour, costing a massive £100 per night. For this I'm getting air and road transport, guides, accommodation and extras such as safari park fees.

Budget is a key factor in booking major tours, and one that clearly divides many travellers I meet. Ajay bears the nickname 'Flashpacker' on the travel websites he contributes to and admits to being financially well off. When travelling to Burma he chose a tailored programme from a professional tour operator to make all his arrangements:

'I was treated like a VIP. The guide had a chauffer-driven car, which displayed the Tour Mandalay board saying "Welcome Dr Ajay to Myanmar". I felt very special. From the cool of the air-conditioned car, I admired the greenness of Rangoon. It was clean, and had orderly traffic, unlike the anarchy and chaos of Delhi and Calcutta. At the hotel we learned that French actor Gerald Depardieu would be coming for a two-night stay tomorrow.'

One of the easiest ways to halve tour costs is of course to share them. Couples on tours will always benefit from shared rooms and halving the costs of luxuries like a car and driver. Charles and Elize's tailored tour of India and Nepal was designed by a UK tour operator to literally cater to their every whim, taking in all the famous luxury hotels and cultural sights they specified. Nevertheless, at around £15,000 each, even the ultimate 10-week honeymoon was a hefty chunk of savings, although they were delighted with almost all of the trip. Their minor criticism of the tour is one that soon becomes familiar when discussing any organised package – just too much travelling:

'We stayed at luxury hotels like the Lake Palace Hotel at Udaipor and beautiful wildlife camps. But a lot of the time we had to fly back to Delhi to transit to the next place. Delhi suffers with chronic fog so often our flights were delayed and we missed half a day. So although we booked top hotels we often didn't arrive until the afternoon. Overall, I would have probably gone to fewer places and spent more time there. You look at a map of India and we barely touched the surface.'

Sometimes taking a tour is the only way to pursue a hobby or interest. Jean and Barry took a lengthy tour to pursue their hobby of playing cricket. Their most recent trip was a 24-day cricket tour of Chile and Argentina in a group of 38 people. After the tour they added a holiday in Brazil:

'The aim was to play cricket-friendly games and go to a festival. All our flights, accommodation and transfers were arranged through the party so we only had to bring along spending money. We all stayed in four- and five-star hotels. We flew business class long haul but I now wish we'd researched the quality of the airlines we took as a group.'

At the budget end of touring, prior to taking his gap year 47-year old Josh had experienced a 28-day coach tour of Europe. It was the core of a longer trip to show his Chinese girlfriend the highpoints of Europe. On turning up in London he realised they were going to be sharing their trip with young Australian backpackers 'doing Europe':

'We decided to just go along with it although we generally felt a bit older and wiser. I'm afraid that didn't last long and most mornings there was a bus full of hungover people reeking of alcohol – including us.

'The best bits were passing through borders, arriving in different countries, and hearing another language. It was January and there was beautiful scenery, stunning lakes and the Swiss Alps. After sunny Spain and the south of France we saw frozen canals in Venice, the beautiful masks, and drank lots of hot chocolate from hands so cold you couldn't work your camera. A lowpoint was drinking too much at the Bierfest in Germany and getting totally lost in a deserted airfield in the snow at 3am. There were other things we'll never forget. Berlin and the Wall were amazing; the Aussies learned more about our history than you'd expect. One *day we stopped at a former concentration camp in Austria in a blizzard. Everyone was very quiet afterwards. It was very, very poignant. On the other hand Amsterdam was totally OTT – live sex shows, spacecakes and joints and getting totally out of it. It was a fantastic once-in-a-lifetime experience. We saw more countries than we could ever have managed on our own – it was a real whirlwind. But you have to be aware of that full-on party culture. It's not going to be for everyone.'*

LAURA'S TIPS: Finding a tour

✓ Most of the major adventure and overland operators have websites that allow you to search for trips by length and specific dates of travel. See the biggest names at www.exodus.co.uk, www.explore.co.uk and www.intrepidtravel.co.uk.

✓ Themed tours such as archaeology, bird-watching, sport or cultural journeys will appeal to more like-minded groups and naturally deepen your cultural understanding of an area.

✓ Personal recommendation is the best guide. Before booking, try to talk to someone who has been on tour with the company.

Day 2 Nairobi, Kenya

My decision to start my round-the-world trip with an organised tour proves to be perfect for me. Once the rest of the group turn up the next day I feel all the responsibility for overseeing every trivial detail of my travel slide effortlessly over onto our guide's shoulders. There are 12 of us in the group and all are women bar one guy, Manuel, who is here with his partner – so any hopes of the single women having holiday romances with a Finch Hatton hunter-type are immediately dashed. Quite a few of the group are travelling alone so there is always someone to talk to and I'm more than happy to be one of the crowd.

We set off in two minibuses up the famous Cairo to Capetown road, dodging baboons to pass boisterous markets and shanties. Almost every other building is a tin-roofed church proclaiming Salvation or Deliverance or, rather more worrying, Healing.

When booking a tour ask...

- Is it cheaper or easier to book a tour or will I enjoy the experience more if I travel independently?

- How far ahead do I need to book? What happens if I cancel? What if insufficient numbers book onto the tour?

- Will I be staying in named hotels or hostels I can check out for reviews?

- How far from the main sights will I be staying?

- What facilities are available, such as bathrooms, laundry or single rooms?

- Is there any free time to do my own thing?

- What extras will I have to pay for, such as tipping, meals, side-trips or taxes?

- Am I fit enough to undertake the trip? (Acclimatisation and general travel malaise will often affect your level of fitness.)

Besides these stridently optimistic slogans are signs of great poverty: *hoteli* eating houses replete with flyblown animal carcasses in the doorway and adverts for suspect medicines. The highway gets worse the further we travel until we finally weave and wobble through yellow dust/smog around potholes the size of quarry pits. Less-fortunate wagons lie overturned by the roadside, their wheels spinning aimlessly like the feeble legs of overturned beetles. Yet by afternoon we're at the comfortably run-down Lake Elementiata Lodge and on a walk with a Maasai guide, Joseph, in his striking red *shuka* cloth. He shows us local herbs and plants and the pink flamingos on the lake. There are by now rippling grey clouds building overhead and then it begins to thunder and rain. I can't believe it – it's only Day Two and already I'm cursing that I've not brought my Pacamac . . .

The independent route

Many gap travellers reject the organised tour option as too regimented. For others it is just too expensive. Sue, 60, took a five-month break alone but found the organised route overpriced:

> 'One tour of New Zealand I wanted to take would have cost more than £3,000 for a week. I did not do it! I might cover the area in a campervan when my husband retires.'

Independent travellers Linda and James left the UK for seven months to tour the world with a couple of backpacks and a determination to have a wonderful time. Taking public transport or hiring campervans, they nevertheless hired occasional guides to take them to places they couldn't reach alone:

> 'We moved to Khao Sok National Park in Thailand and took a guide for the most amazing trip. We started at the man-made massive lake on a longtail boat for a ride through amazing, huge limestone karsts (like mountains but more sheer) surrounded by

monkeys and hornbills. Then we went on a three-hour trek through the jungle with our guide into some incredible under-ground caves. Some were filled with water – sometimes deeper than me – so we had to swim through. James and the guide had head-lights because it was pitch black; for me it was pretty scary but also amazing. Then we went to a row of huts by the lake where we stayed overnight and had our own little veranda right onto the lake. We ate the best Thai food there – green curry and sweet and sour plus fresh fish cooked in red chillies. The next morning we jumped into the lake straight from bed – better than a warm shower. And then we went canoeing. We had the best time ever – so beautiful and peaceful – and as we drank a beer on our veranda at sunset, we toasted everyone we knew back at home hard at work.'

Travelling under your own steam has its own special highs. There is the freedom and the pleasure of making it up as you go along. It allows for serendipity – an extra week at that beautiful guesthouse in a forest or having time to travel somewhere unexpected with a new friend.

Gilly, 64, fulfilled a lifetime ambition to travel to New Zealand via a visit to her daughter in Los Angeles. A highlight for Gilly and her husband Ken was to get off the main tour routes and interact with the locals:

'I planned the itinerary and accommodation. We stayed in mostly B&B homestays plus one or two motels. We were not disap-pointed. By staying in homestays we were given information about the area and secret spots to get off the beaten track. When we were in Kinloch by Lake Taupo we were told about the Forgotten Highway, a wonderful route to New Plymouth. We were told that only 2% of New Zealanders knew about it. This is the kind of information that was given us by our hosts. We prefer exploring off the tourist route.'

LAURA'S TIPS: Taking the independent route

Long tours can leave you feeling trapped in the same group day after day, rankled by crazy schedules that pass in a blur. Instead you opt for complete freedom to travel where you want and when you want. But remember the independent route can take bucketloads of patience and resilience:

✓ From the moment you get off the plane each destination can present a challenge of orientation and finding accommodation. Try to pre-book at least your first night's rest.

✓ Be prepared for more time than you expect to be spent obtaining transport, accommodation and simply finding your way around.

✓ Hiring a multilingual guide can be money well spent to help you meet locals and get to less-visited areas.

A place to stay

Our travellers stayed in a vast variety of accommodation: mud huts, campervans, tents, rented villas, treehouses and boats. As a major cost of the trip, many travellers do their utmost to stay in reasonable places at the lowest cost. The low prices left Kate and Keith enthusiastic:

'In Bali hotels are very cheap and negotiable at the moment owing to the government warnings which I totally oppose. We ended up

staying in very nice accommodation at really good prices (£20 max a night). In Australia and New Zealand we used backpacker places, which are everywhere and by and large really good, though you do get the odd bad place. We started out staying in dorms but in the end paid a bit extra for a double room – I think at 40 there is a limit to your tolerance of other people's sleeping/sexual pattern of behaviour! Thai hotels, houses and guesthouses varied from £30 per night to £2.50. We found that good accommodation could be found cheaply once on the ground – we averaged about £10 per night.'

Most independent travellers invest in one of the two major guide books to world travel and use these as a catalogue of accommodation. Career breaker Paul, 31, spent a year touring Australia and New Zealand:

'During my year away I stayed in approximately 45 different locations, mostly hostels and occasionally just for one night. Accommodation was generally excellent. A little bit of planning and a guide book are essential. I only stayed at three hostels in a year that I thought were poor and each of those employed backpackers as central members of staff. You also need to be aware of the migration patterns of backpackers in Australia – everybody wants to be in Sydney for the New Year, in Melbourne in March for the Grand Prix, and up north (or west) when it's colder in May to August. The predictability of this movement is very similar to migrating birds! If you want a bed in a Sydney hostel for New Year you need to book very, very early – about two months ahead.'

Mary-Ann and Michael travel for three months every year using the Rough Guide. Michael insists that it's preferable to use an impartial guide book to asking around in a country like Sri Lanka:

'We stay in very low-level guest houses living amongst the locals in their own environment, usually on the beach where I can fish.

THE FACTS: Accommodation

Wherever you stay will have a major bearing on your level of comfort – and, naturally, your budget. Remember that once on the road choices will be infinitely greater and bargains can be found by asking around:

- **Hotels** – services should be good but you may feel 'cocooned' from the culture you have travelled to see.

- **Hostels** – no longer simply fetid dorms, many have double en suite rooms at bargain prices. There is no age limit to stay in a hostel (for International Youth Hostels see www.hihostels.com).

- **Guesthouses and B&Bs** – vary from upmarket mini-hotels to a basic room in a family home. Ask to see the room before booking.

- **Homestays** – run by people who offer a bedroom in their home to guests. A great way to gain cultural insights but the lack of privacy can be a strain.

- **Camping** – either free camping outside towns or on camp sites. Walk-in tents with camp beds are a great option if you don't want to hump the gear about.

- **Farmstays** – some upmarket farms offer language courses in a rural setting (www.farmstays.org) while others provide work on farms (no age limit but must be fit and healthy). See World-Wide Opportunities on Organic Farms (www.wwoof.org).

- **House swaps** – register with an agency to swap your house for another one at your destination (see www.homelink.org.uk).

- **Alternative living** – while not mainstream tourist accommoda-tion, bed and board is offered at some spiritual retreats such as the international community Auroville in India (www.auroville.org). See the directory of international com-munities for a range of alternative communities (www.ic.org).

Living like that gives a true taste of the country you are visiting. Be wary of people who approach you to sell accommodation and tours as they are generally more expensive. Do look around. You can generally find a clean room with hot water and en suite for well under £10 per night.'

Any initial worries Fran had about staying in hostels geared up for young backpackers soon disappeared when she found them much friendlier than the B&Bs where older people usually stay. In Bali she found the bargain hotel she had booked on the internet was way beyond her expectations:

'I went to see my room. Oh, wow. This beautiful room, this huge bed and all these flowers on my pillow. My bathroom full of flowers. It was lovely. They made such beautiful breakfasts every morning. Fruit, and eggs in different ways, always so pretty. I was there 11 days and had the time of my life. I was ruined!'

Older travellers have far more contacts than their younger counterparts so, unsurprisingly, many use the trip to catch up with friends and family around the world. Old school friends, workmates and distant relatives can all be called on to offer their sofas and spare rooms. On Sue's trip to the Antipodes she managed to include house-sitting and even a house swap. Abby's tour of eastern Europe also called on contacts through her Polish stepfather who organised a raft of relatives to stay with:

'I stayed in people's houses in Berlin, Vienna, Budapest, Prague, Warsaw and Krakow. It gave me the chance to see how people lived and get a deeper connection with the people and places.'

Rather than book rooms by the night, the long-term traveller can also look for a house or apartment to rent when they want to settle down for a while in an interesting place. Spending a few months in Thailand, Kate and Keith found their perfect house, not only for themselves but as a place to invite friends:

'The villa was fantastic, up in the mountains with a great view and infinity pool – the works. To top it off, I could sit on the veranda with a cup of tea and email to my heart's content. We have realised that internet access and a cup of tea are core to our travelling stability. It was lovely to have a little home for a while – we are renting it again when our friends come over.'

On the other hand, you can always bring your own roof to put over your head. Sue and her two sons packed a tent and found it ideal for children:

'If I completed this trip again I would definitely camp more often. We would have done so in Canada had the weather been better. I wouldn't book accommodation in advance although everyone thought I was crazy not to. It is more exciting not knowing where you are going to be and as long as you have a tent you always have an option. I think I would kit us up fully for camping next time. We could also have saved a lot of money by cooking for ourselves.'

Don't forget that by taking the completely independent route there will be times when the sheer difficulty and time-consuming nature of getting about may get you down. Particularly when alone, there can be logistical issues about getting you and your luggage around. When 50-year-old Joanne backpacked with her son George, she occasionally found travelling long distances on a small budget tiresome:

'I think you do forget the heat, frustration and maddeningly slow pace of a lot of it. On a really tight budget you spend a lot of time hanging around bus terminals and waiting for offices to open. That's when it's really helpful to be in a couple, so one can look after the bags while the other does the business like buying tickets or checking out a room. On the other hand, when you negotiate a great beach bungalow or out-of-season hotel with pool for a few pounds a night it's a really great feeling. You also meet some *incredible fellow travellers. Having said that, I don't think I'd actually backpack again.'*

Patience, patience, patience – that's the advice I hear again and again to budget travellers using local transport and hostels. It's this ability to slow right down to the local pace of life that some travellers talk about with genuine nostalgia on their return and others find just maddening. Be prepared for things to go wrong, backtracking and failed arrangements are the price to be paid for those wonderful moments of serendipity the independent traveller can happen upon.

Emrys stayed in Ghanaian village houses while working on projects but confessed he was used to travelling on a shoestring:

'I'm used to just having a bedroll, a sleeping sheet and a mosquito net. I preferred to stay somewhere with a tin roof than thatch because of the rats. Having said that, it would have mud floors and basic furniture but was always kept clean.'

In Asia, personal trainer Josh took the cheapest budget route and discovered accommodation redolent with local atmosphere:

'In Vietnam I lived in a colourful apartment with a terrace at the top to enjoy Saigon's skyline. I was surrounded by twisting alleyways, the smell of noodles, babies crying on doorsteps, families lounging on mats in front of the TV, and every so often an old wizened face smoking a pipe would peer around my door.'

Also experiencing life in the raw was volunteer Polly, 53. Being close to a squatter camp in South Africa, her living conditions were basic but always lively:

'The house was pretty basic and there were volunteers from all over the world working on various projects in the village, so the house was pretty lively with about 12 people living communally. I

lived in a little cottage apart from the main house, with a little bedroom, a bathroom and a veranda, close enough to the main house for safety but far enough for some peace and quiet.

'I got a lot of visitors, plenty of snakes and spiders, and you quickly learn which ones are to be avoided. The smallest spiders are the most deadly so checking your bed before climbing into it is always a good idea, likewise your shoes before slipping your bare feet into them! Baboons were the most regular and unwelcome visitors. They were ever present in the trees about 20ft from the cottage and groups of them regularly made raids on the house.'

Yet it's the contact with the local community that can be the making of your trip and travelling independently means you'll get personal with the local people – and the wildlife – all the way. So if you're prepared for a rollercoaster of highs and lows, dirt, dust and raw but beautiful experiences, the independent route is for you.

Day 5 Maasai Mara, Kenya

Sometimes the beauty of a tour is that the experts get you straight to the right place at the right time. Seeing animals in the wild is a world away from any David Attenborough documentary. Firstly, there is the hyper-reality of being in petting distance of utterly wild and beautiful creatures. As a family of elephants lumber towards us we can virtually feel the breeze waft from their flapping ears. Standing a few feet from a white rhino there's such a bristling atmosphere that I challenge anyone to be shaken out of their usual holiday daze. Then there is the sheer abundance of game: whole armies of zebras and wildebeest, pools teeming with hippos and crocodiles and lakes blurry pink with flamingos.

We are just in time for one of the world's great spectacles – The Migration. Wildebeest arrive at the river's edge in a great army of bobbing horns atop tinderstick legs. Uncertain, they halt en masse, groaning and pawing the ground. Finally a few brave leaders scramble down the rocks and splash into the water. Others follow until a black string like wooden beads crosses from bank to bank. 'There's a crocodile,' our guide Davis whispers. I can't see it but peer anxiously at the vulnerable beasts hopping from rock to rock. Suddenly one beast is separated from the herd. Bellowing, he stumbles and struggles, fighting off underwater teeth and jaws. The herd backs off and he is utterly alone now, flailing in the bloody froth, pawing and slipping on rocks that offer no purchase to his weakened limbs. It is a slow and horrible death as five crocodiles pull him down to their underwater larder. You wanted to see wildlife, the Mara seems to say – well here it is in all its gore and glory.

CULTURE SHOCK

Day 6 Maasai Mara, Kenya

Approaching Kenya's vast game reserve, the Maasai Mara, I had already been captivated by glimpses of barefoot Maasai herders, their red or purple *shuka* cloths tied over their shoulders, staffs in hand, herding cattle across a landscape dotted with flat-topped acacia trees. Maasai women also roam the wide-skied landscape: tall and agile figures in turquoise or orange cloaks, striding fast with switches in their hands, their babies' heads bobbing in slings tied across their backs.

Our guide, Davis, tells us that the Maasai people are one of the last nomadic tribes of East Africa, whereas many of his own people, the Kikuyu, have now settled in one place. Famous as fiercely independent warriors, the Maasai cling to their traditional way of life, despite insistent pressures to adopt a more conventional lifestyle. The fact is that the Maasai now have less than a quarter of the territory they held before Europeans arrived and one of the few options left to them to support their way of life is tourism and acting out the role of the 'noble savage'.

The village we visit is a circle of mud huts inside a thorn fence where the villagers' prized cattle are corralled every night. The entrance fee is $10 donated towards schooling for the children and in return we take photographs freely. The stunning women dressed in rainbow costumes decorated with beaded collars and headbands greet us with a song of welcome. Despite faces alive with crawling flies and the crunch of dried dung underfoot my impression is of happy and jokey people. Even the wiry 'Old Mama' giggles and shrieks at her image on my digital camera screen. I'm keen to explore a mud-baked hut and it is as dark as a cellar inside as I feel my way down narrow corridors to find two sleeping places and a stone fireplace just like a Bronze Age cooking hearth. I don't see any evidence of their most famous food, a mixture of cow's blood and milk, but later do see the gashes on the neck of cattle that Davis tells us are bled to feed the warriors as they traverse the land. As we leave it's easy to feel that a show has been put on for us tourists, for how authentic can a meeting like this really be? After all, most of us westerners are only here for a few weeks and barely scratch the surface of a country.

Tim has strong views on tourism and its potential damage to local economies and cultures:

> 'Don't try to change the lives of the people; you are there to change your own life. Do not have preconceived ideas. Different countries do things differently, it's their way. If you don't like it, leave.'

The sad reality is that in some places the scourge of tourism has already left a nasty scar. It could be a strip of bars and nightclubs that destroys a traditional fishing village. Or it could be depressing tours to see tribal people dressed up and performing 'to camera'. Sometimes it stares you in the face, like Joanne's observations in Bali:

THE GROWN UP GAP YEAR DIARIES

LAURA'S TIPS: Eco-travel

Having arrived in a unique culture the last thing an enlightened traveller wants to do is damage it. Sensible advice on responsible tourism focuses on simple behaviour changes to minimise the impact of tourism:

✓ Be informed about local politics and customs. Guide books are one source but novels, biographies and local newspapers can provide a much deeper understanding.

✓ Stay in locally owned hotels and guesthouses and use local guides and transport.

✓ Conserve resources by being careful with water, fuel and electricity. Don't dump litter, and refill your water bottles.

✓ Whenever you can, shop locally and buy local products. Don't become obsessed with haggling or finding the best deals.

✓ Respect local customs, religions and traditions. Dress appropriately and make an effort to learn at least a few words of the local language.

✓ Ask for permission before photographing people.

'When we got to Bali it was impossible not to notice the rubbish, and especially heaps of plastic water bottles around the beaches. Thankfully, I hear there is now a much-needed trend towards refillable water siphons in cafés and hotels but it can't happen too soon. Bali just doesn't have the resources to deal with all that plastic.'

Only on one occasion in Kenya do I feel painfully uncomfortable about our presence in the natural idyll of a game reserve. We are in search of a leopard that has been sighted near our camp. Only today it's not just our two minibuses on the trail, but a host of other jeeps carrying tourists from Japan, Italy and the UK that lurch in a ragged procession across the rutted grassland. Unsurprisingly, given all this racket, the leopard is hiding up a tree. It's completely camouflaged with the biological assistance of its spots, the only creature with dignity in a thicket of craning necks and clicking cameras. Soon it is caged in by diesel-plumed vehicles, their suspensions groaning and engines rumbling like tanks. I want nothing to do with this and feel terribly guilty.

There are few black and white issues in this eco-debate but one benefit of eco-tourism should be a greater awareness of environmental issues in those returning to the west. Whether it's a new understanding of water conservation, of community values or just how few possessions are needed to live a contented and useful life, a period of travelling can profoundly change your outlook. Many older travellers find it harder to justify the hedonistic 'one long party' that many younger gappers take and seek out active engagement with local people. Volunteering to help local communities is one way of giving back something to the world that especially appeals to older travellers. Becoming an overseas volunteer is rarely easy but often rewarding. It can also be fraught with controversy, as a backlash has arisen against rich westerners becoming gap year volunteers, earning the label the 'new colonialism'.

Qualified in soil and water engineering, 42-year-old Emrys helped set up his own charity with four other people through a student trust. It took a couple of years to come to fruition and was intended to give opportunities for anyone to help out:

> 'The reason we chose Ghana was because English is their lingua franca. Obviously if you're going to teach people, there's no point in going to a country with all the skills but no way of communicating. We had a Range Rover with a trailer and an 18-tonne truck. So my packing was things like a lathe, a milling machine and about three tonnes of tools. I was teaching people soil conservation techniques, water collection, composting, pit latrines, whatever they needed. We weren't going over there to tell them how to do something, but if they asked how to dig a well we showed them how to do it. It was their project not ours. Far too much development aid is self fulfilling, giving the charity workers a job for life.'

Another impressive volunteer is Polly, a textile designer whose work has brought valuable benefits to a rural squatter camp in South Africa. Taking on work organised by Willing Workers in South Africa (www.wwisa.co.za) she worked in highly challenging conditions:

> 'The homes in the camp are ramshackle shacks built of scrap wood, rusty corrugated metal and even piles of cardboard. The social problems are heartbreaking: poverty, alcohol abuse, drugs, domestic violence and, sadly, child abuse. Unemployment is 70%, with little hope of work.

> 'I began very slowly, letting them see me work and building up a trust base. One of the more vocal ladies of the group agreed to let me work with her. Helen does fabric painting. Technically she's OK but her subject matter and choice of colour were diabolical. I

did a few simple African-style designs and put some groups of colour together for her and soon her first set of cushions were ready for the shop. To Helen's delight they sold within three hours and for twice the price she would normally ask. That was good for Helen but even better for me as it was my passport in to the ladies. One by one they quietly asked if I would help them with their product. So now it's full on; at the moment I've got projects well under way with seven of the group and I'm about to start with three more. Knitting, weaving, fabric painting, mosaics, basketry, patchwork – the place has turned into a little hive of activity.'

Voluntary work

Find out as much as you can about the day to day realities of any volunteer work:

- How will your work benefit the local people in the long term?

- What will you be expected to do all day?

- How closely does this match your skills?

- Who else will be there?

- Can you talk to former volunteers about their experience?

- What will the accommodation and other facilities be like?

- What health precautions do you need to take?

- How much time will you have to yourself to travel and look around?

- What happens if you don't want to complete the placement?

Many gap travellers choose a specialist gap organisation to put together a spell as a volunteer. The result is a new and very mixed industry that will package together 'experiences' of every kind, from marine biology in the Pacific to working with orphans in India. What should be a laudable service is nevertheless littered with controversy as I find out when I meet grown-up gapper and orphanage volunteer Alex.

First of all, there is the price. Alex, a smart 37-year-old, paid £1,100 for a month's experience teaching AIDS orphans in Zambia. Fed up and disillusioned after decades of work, she wrote a list of her life's dreams including working with orphans, taking a tour to meet gorillas, experiencing the Rio Carnival and sailing on a tall ship from New Zealand to Easter Island. After several attempts to negotiate time off from her media job she eventually negotiated a six-month career break. At a proposed budget of £16,000, Alex's gap experience is a real once-in-a-lifetime splurge, one of the more expensive trips I come across. Like many gappers she found her building society unhelpful when she told them she wanted to rent out her flat while travelling. In the end she decided to let a friend 'house-sit' rather than set up a full-blown tenancy agreement.

As Alex's story reveals, volunteering can be fraught with difficult moral dilemmas:

> 'I used a well-known gap year organisation to sort out my voluntary placement. First of all, they didn't even meet me at the airport. It was run by very young and incompetent kids. The security was terribly lax – other volunteers had goods stolen and one bunch of youngsters were mugged. Some of the other volunteers just went home when they saw how badly managed it was.

> 'I had chosen this particular provider because I didn't want to do building or painting in the afternoons. Yet I was immediately expected to do it. I refused and offered extra teaching instead.

When I did turn up to teach, the teacher walked out so I was forced to teach for the whole month. The rewards were fantastic, the kids were incredible and I loved them. They wrote me letters and bought me a present which was terribly moving as they are so poor. But I don't know if the teacher ever came back. I don't know what I think about it now.'

When the volunteer's skills and enthusiasm match the project, truly great things are achieved. When Polly returned to South Africa a year later she found the perfect end to her work:

'I returned to the project I was working on to see how they are progressing and was greatly heartened to see that they don't really need me any more. The gallery I set up is a success and the ladies have kept it looking good and also the orders for work are rolling in.'

It is not only travellers on long voluntary work placements who return with a deeper understanding of environmental issues. By spending time in another culture, many other travellers discover new perspectives and insights. Sue, on her post-retirement trip to the Antipodes, talks of helping in a rural community:

'At one point I volunteered to clear gorse in Tasmania. It's considered a pest which kills natives – and the British planted it! I also learned a lot about water conservation and how to cook and clean in different ways to save water.'

Giving something back to local people, however small, can often be the highlight of a trip. Michael and Mary-Ann encountered problems in Sri Lanka as the country teetered on the edge of civil war. But none of their difficulties could take away the pleasure of helping children in a troubled country:

'The highlight for me was a small children's day school for the poor and seeing their faces on our return the next day with bags of milk powder and pens and paper for them to draw on.'

An increasingly militarised society disturbed Michael and Mary-Ann, but where do you stand on taking a holiday in what may be considered a military dictatorship? Are you helping the people by spending your tourist money, even if their government does not allow what we call a free society? Burma is a controversial destination since the pro-democracy leader Aung San Suu Kyi appealed to foreigners to boycott her country. Nevertheless, Ajay decided to visit Burma and made all his bookings through a private Rangoon-based tour operator. On arrival he found out what life in a repressed society feels like:

> 'People won't talk about politics, democracy and the pro-democracy leader Aung San Suu Kyi. There were few mobile phones, no internet as we know it and no free press or TV. I learnt first hand what a military dictatorship is and felt oppressed after the 10th day. But I still say go to Burma. Always engage private tour operators, spend money in private hotels, restaurants, private airlines and private buses. In this way one puts money, jobs, bread and butter into the common man's world and can provide and sustain employment and livelihoods. I only gave a $20 visa fee to the government and another $10 to the government hotel in Lashio. I have no moral regrets in visiting Burma.'

Day 7 Nairobi, Kenya

My time lurking in the safe haven of an organised tour is nearing its end. And with perfect timing I'm facing my first mini-crisis. The blue rucksack on wheels that has given me the heebie-jeebies since my husband persuaded me to buy it has burst at the seams. Tomorrow I fly to Zanzibar and I don't think it will survive the flight. I need a new bag and I need it fast.

I consider shopping in Nairobi on my own but I've been listening to Paul Theroux's account of his African odyssey, *Dark Star Safari*

(Penguin 2003) on mp3, and even he is intimidated by the city's reputation. So I decide to throw cash at the problem and hire a taxi to take me to the store entrance. In the end, my friendly driver insists he sticks by my side like a bodyguard. There are armed security guards around the store and, as I anticipated, I really do seem to be the only white woman in town. It all works out well in the end. I'm £80 worse off after buying the sturdiest wheelie bag I can find, while I transfer the storepoints from the transaction towards my driver's Christmas shopping. I can hardly believe how relieved I am to have a decent bag. Oh, and I now have room for souvenirs. My blood pressure has dropped from Panic to Chilled Out in half an hour.

Day 8 Stonetown, Zanzibar, Tanzania

"The loveliest city in Africa", says my guidebook of Stonetown, Zanzibar – so my expectations are high. They are soon dashed by damp-blackened walls and alleys heaped with rubbish. Yes, there are eerie palaces and labyrinthine alleys but much of the city is tainted with mildew and centuries of decay. Not for the first time I feel a twitch of culture shock. Dirt, mould, things that crawl – I'm feeling uneasy and out of kilter. I see something scurry behind the wardrobe of my Arabian-style hotel room – please let it only be a lizard and not something that likes to nibble on sleeping humans in the dark.

Zanzibar market fills my eyes, ears and nose with the exotic. It's a cacophony of reggae sound systems, touts, stinking fishsellers and infinitely graceful women in orange, green and blue *kangas* draped around plump, serene faces. Back in the alleys outdoor televisions hold groups of men entranced – it's Everton *v.* Fulham and chalkboards detail fixtures and tips. But the key to this strange outpost of spices and Islam is the slave market beside the blackened spire of the cathedral. Here in this edgy, neglected former outpost of the

🌍 THE FACTS: Culture shock

Culture shock is a form of anxiety produced by a new environment that strikes many travellers as they move in and out of different cultures:

- Symptoms include low mood, difficulty sleeping and preoccupation with health.

- The stages of culture shock can pass between a honeymoon period when everything is new and exciting to various phases of dissatisfaction, realisation and, finally, integration when good and bad things about the new culture are recognised.

- The final phase of re-entry on returning home at the end of the trip can be equally intense and trigger feelings of not belonging.

- Ways to help counter culture shock include relaxation and meditation, learning the language, allowing yourself to feel homesick and generally being easier on yourself as you adapt to a different way of life.

Omani sultans I clamber down to two underground hollows formerly used as human containers for slaves. My heart sinks to witness the ancient chains inside coffin-like darkness.

Alcohol is banned in all but a few licensed bars but as we eat at a cheery café, the owner surreptitiously supplies red wine in Coke bottles and white in Sprite. We could almost be in Europe beside any moonlit ocean. Then our hostess rushes out with shrieks and a waving broom. It's a rat: fat, brown and fearless, boldly surfaced from the street.

Modern travel moves us so rapidly from culture to culture that it's hardly surprising our emotions are buffeted. Sometimes it's not just the poverty but the sheer extremes of wealth and values that shock us. On her travels, 70-year-old Fran was not impressed when moving from Hong Kong to Sydney:

'I heard about the people who live in stilt houses on Lantau Island and a man offered to show me around in return for me treating him to tea. Oh the poverty – I was nearly in tears. But it was about ten in the morning and they were all gambling and playing mah jong and drinking. My heart went out to them but there's not a lot you can do about it, just passing through. I suppose the biggest culture shock was that two days later I'm on a Sydney Harbour tour and all they're telling me about these multi-millionaire houses. And 48 hours before there are these poor people living in huts on stilts over a river.'

Backpackers Kate and Keith began their visit to Cambodia with a strong inclination to meet the local people. They befriended their tuk-tuk driver and found his family warm and welcoming. But after a few weeks the heat, difficult conditions and summer colds had got to Kate:

'My love affair with Cambodia swiftly came to an end – if it ever started. Too much poverty, corruption and pollution (plastic bags are the scourge of the world). We had a bizarre experience when we arrived – a copper was beating the tuk-tuk drivers off with a stick to allow us to disembark off the bus. All of them wanted the fare with the older white folks (us) rather than the backpacker young ones. Angkor Wat was nice to see but the killing fields were horrid. You realise after about 10 minutes that the paths you are walking on actually have bones and cloth coming to the surface.

'And our hotel room was shit – the bed was small, old and took the shape of a banana when you got in it. We could have moved to another place but you try carrying 20kg in that heat in search of accommodation. So that was us – sitting in a stinking hotel in

40°C temperatures with a cold and surrounded by beggars and aggressive tuk-tuk drivers. I have tremendous respect for all the younger travellers doing "south-east Asia on a shoestring" but it wasn't for me.'

Day 11 Jambiani, Zanzibar, Tanzania

Our first impressions of Jambiani village are of roofless ruins and ramshackle coral and lime huts set back from the western-style hotels that hug the beach. Despite a little apprehension I'm keen to find out what life is like for our close neighbours. As this final part of our tour has no guide I seek out a village tour run by a local cultural organisation to promote cultural understanding. Six of my Exodus group come along as Mr Rama, a courteous young man eager to improve his English, leads us through the scorching sunshine among throngs of sturdy black toddlers clamouring to be swung by their chubby arms. Later I meet children barely a year or two older working on the beaches, filling sacks with seaweed. It's a way for the local women and children to earn a wage but they tell me their income is always falling from the seaweed, that is eventually exported to Japan for sushi.

At the village kindergarten neat and lively children wear uniforms of lilac shirts and, for the girls, modest lilac headscarves. The children learn three languages: Arabic, Swahili and English, and we are treated to an exuberant version of 'One Two, How Are You?' Amongst them, three women teachers sit on the floor in dark robes with henna patterned hands. Lastly, Mr Soloman, the herbal medicine man, explains his craft with a demonstration of the roots and leaves that he and his forbears have prescribed for ailments for the last four generations. Mr Rama tells us there is no crime in the village and a powerful community project has recently eradicated malaria and set up sewing and planting projects.

At the suggestion of a local charity I've brought a batch of books as gifts for local schools: *The Arabian Nights* in English. It's a carefully chosen book both in its Islamic religious context and its irresistible seafaring characters. I suggest to Mr Rama that the school might want a copy but his eyes brighten as he reverentially inspects it. He himself is learning English, he confides. Perhaps he might read it first and pass it on? It's a pleasure to see his delight as he carefully packs the book in his shoulder bag. Rather than a tip of money, I feel that Scheherazade and her thousand and one tales create something like a fair exchange. In return for the book I've learned that this predominantly Muslim village is keen to do the best for its families and their future – and is nowhere to be frightened of at all.

Day 13 Pongwe, Zanzibar, Tanzania

As a treat Pongwe Beach Hotel has it all. The food is wonderful, the beach a vision of crystal white sand rippling to various shades of aqua and turquoise lagoon. It also has lots of those small touches to make your stay special: a beach bag complete with towels and sarong, morning tea, lazy hammocks and clean, fresh bathrooms with proper hot showers. It claims to be eco-friendly, too. Bliss. At last I can indulge my original fantasy of beach life with three glorious days of downtime and then it's time to move on. Tomorrow I start for Cochin in southern India. Another day, another continent!

GOING SOLO

Day 16 Cochin, India

James, my driver, is waiting for me in Cochin in a smart white uniform beside his spotless white Ambassador car. He's a bizarre contrast to me in my bare-toed sandals and trekking trousers. Cruising over to my hotel, James frowns and complains, 'This is not a very good hotel. More like a homestay.' My decision to spend the majority of my time in basic hotels and homestays is based on my wish to meet local people, taste their food and absorb the spirit of different places. I don't want to sit in a concrete box run by a western chain. I can't help but feel I'm something of a disappointment to my crisply laundered driver.

Nevertheless, I begin to feel rather lonely in Cochin. It reminds me of a northern British city with its sari-wearing mothers, Asian-accented English and pushy young street vendors. The big difference is that over here the people appear so much more relaxed: happy family groups promenading in the street striving to outdo each other in the brightest saris (women) and most bouffant hair-dos (men). I stare at them; they stare at me. The most frequent question is: 'Where are your family?'

Day 17 Cochin, India

I decide that one of the pleasures of solo travel must be to please myself entirely. So I stop hiding in my hotel's restaurant and dine alone at the most interesting restaurant in town. The History Restaurant at the Brunton Boatyard traces the influence of succeeding invaders on Keralan food: from Portuguese stews and Dutch pancakes to British mutton curries.

I book a lone table and return self-conscious and overdressed in the evening. The kindly waiters help me kick off with Keralan green prawns, fresh and hot with a fiery green mango chutney. Next, I'm guided to a Syrian dish of braised duck with rice flour noodles. It's lusciously tender and spiced with cardamom, pepper and chunks of sweet cinnamon bark. To end, I go off menu. Do they have kulfi ice cream? Mango kulfi arrives and it is rich and creamy and shot through with strands of saffron. It is a wonderful meal and all for less than £10.

To cap it all I wander back to my cheap but lovely hotel to enjoy one of those magical moments that you have to be alone to enjoy fully. I'm staying in one of the oldest buildings in Cochin and my spacious creaky room is at the top of a dark polished stairway that overlooks the cool central courtyard. Tonight three musicians are playing classical Indian music by lamplight down in the courtyard. Leaning on the balustrade, inhaling the scents of the night, I listen to the flute soar and swoop like a mythical bird around the ancient walls. I sigh and think to myself that this is a little epiphany: a sudden illumination that I'm actually here in this wonderful place, fully grasping this precious moment in my life. For that insight, being alone is a fair price.

Travelling alone

For many older gap travellers a huge attraction is to take time out alone. After decades of work, childcare and people-pleasing, the lure of solitary travel is irresistible. The lone traveller can linger as long as they choose, please themselves every day and move on or hang around as the fancy takes them. There's also something about being utterly alone that intensifies the travel experience and allows us to think those deep thoughts that may have been stifled for years. The beauty of the landscape can be more fully appreciated and photography and journal writing can become less of a duty and more of a meditation.

Fran was certain that she was going to celebrate her 70th year by travelling alone. She wanted to feel untrammelled by friends' interests and agendas that might divert her from her main interests: taking long walks and appreciating the natural landscape:

> *'I couldn't go with anyone else. My friend would want to go round the shops and I'd probably join her while I really wanted to go on a walk for miles and miles on my own. Yes, there are times when you think – I wish I could have said to somebody, "Look up there, just look at that." But you know, they might not appreciate it. I might think it's beautiful and they might think – "Oh, that's only a white flower."*

Mid-life and later life are times when many of us feel the need to stand back and re-evaluate our lives. A period of travelling away from family and ordinary pressures can be a liberating chance to reflect on the past and future. Still fit and healthy, too mentally active to retire, many mature gappers search out the stimulus of new experiences and vistas.

When Tim sold his boat to drive off to Morocco his goal was to be alone:

'*It was time to rest, recuperate and start to look after my mind, body and soul. Time to think of me, to be selfish, after spending a life thinking of everyone else first. And to try to decide what to do with the rest of my life. I am still young! I went on my own and met a huge number of people on the way. Being on my own, it was easy to choose who I did or didn't want to spend time with. I also wanted to have plenty of time with just me and my thoughts, to think through my future without any outside influence at all. It was always a pleasure to be alone, and never a problem (unless I had a language problem with nobody to assist).*'

Solo travellers often point out that if they feel lonely it's easy to befriend fellow travellers. While locals are often wary of approaching couples or groups, a single person is more likely to make friends and learn about the locality. And once they tire of their new companions they can move on without having to compromise.

Abby had intended to meet a German friend to tour eastern Europe by train but her friend failed to turn up. It left Abby with a choice – cancel the trip or go on ahead:

'*When my German friend couldn't make it I was waiting to meet her in Sofia, Bulgaria. I felt very let down and disappointed. But then I decided to explore the city on my own and stayed in a homestay with a kind elderly couple. I spent five days in Sofia and visited the Ottoman treasures, the churches and museums and discovered a wonderful city. I found out how liberating travelling on my own is. I didn't realise how much I'd love it and how people are drawn to solo travellers. Many people came to chat to me so I never really felt alone.*'

Particularly on the well-worn backpacker trails outlined in the major guidebooks, you will never be far from other Europeans doing similar trips to yourself. Paul, taking a year out to work and travel around Australia, soon found that travelling alone was never going to be lonely:

'I met many, many people in the year away. For the most part I travelled by myself and met heaps of people. In fact I actually think it's harder to meet people when you are in a group because lone travellers tend to mix with each other and are wary of groups.'

Going solo – pros and cons

Pros

- Being alone creates a more intense, deeply personal experience.
- You have time to learn about your own motivations, likes and dislikes.
- Meeting people can be easier and more natural.
- It's an opportunity to do your own thing to your own time agenda.
- You are far more likely to 'live your dream' than if you compromise with another person's itinerary and interests.

Cons

- In difficult situations it's just you and your wits sorting it out.
- Two cope better with practical issues like minding luggage or getting help if one person falls ill.
- You can have difficulties shaking off unwanted companions.
- Culture shock and loneliness can hit harder.
- All lone travellers need to take extra note of Foreign Office warnings: to avoid chaotic festivals and demonstrations, for example.

Of course there are disadvantages to travelling alone. There are security risks, especially when tired or disorientated. In particular, it is important not to carry too much luggage and to do your best to blend in with local dress and behaviours. Yet as Polly says of her trips to Africa:

> 'I always travel alone. It is sometimes lonely, but the advantages overcome that.'

Women alone

Seventy percent of all solo travellers are now women. Women today know they are the first generation who can do virtually all they want to do. They have education, money and a sense of adventure. If you as a lone woman choose to take a look around Australia, the USA or northern Europe and the chances are that no one will single you out as unusual. But in less-developed nations where family networks are paramount you may be viewed as something of an oddity. Like an old scratched record you will be asked a hundred times a day where your husband and family are and what they think of you travelling alone. Even the most ardent feminists have been known to relent and slip on a gold ring and invent a husband just to discourage unwanted questions – and admirers.

Most lone women travellers are never physically attacked but hassle is fairly commonplace. This could range from unwanted flirting to groping in crowds or offensive remarks or gestures. The consensus is that the best response is to stay cool and get away from the source of the hassle as quickly and confidently as you can. On her rail trip, solo traveller Abby occasionally encountered offensive men:

> 'On a very full train to Bratislava there was a middle-aged man who leered and made sexual gestures to me. Even though other

people on the train told him off he still ogled me during the whole trip and it was rather unnerving as he was a nasty, lecherous character.'

In some countries like the Caribbean, Africa and Indonesia, your lone status may lead local gigolos to think you are in search of romance. Again, an imaginary husband and friendly refusal is usually enough to put them off. If you are interested in romance with a local in a developing country proceed with extreme caution. AIDS is a very real risk and the emotional consequences of paying for attention and sex (which is what your romance will probably boil down to) can be horribly painful.

Joanne soon became aware that there were plenty of 'Kuta Cowboys' on Bali keen to pay attention to older western women:

'I personally ignored them but got to know one woman and her boyfriend very well. She was in her 40s, divorced and attractive and was very much on a sex holiday. She paid for everything while her attractive young Balinese boyfriend was staying with her. She was very cool and down to earth about the whole thing. It was the younger backpackers who were shocked and complained about the noise from their bedroom – noisy sex all night, every night, seemed to be the arrangement.'

Day 18 Tellicherry, India

Taking the long, chaotic road up to Tellicherry reveals that Kerala is certainly not just Bradford or Bolton plus sunshine. In 1957 Kerala became the first state in the world to form an elected communist government (with the exception of the Italian principality of San Marino). I head to the 'Moscow' of the state, Pinarayi, which is still under Marxist control. The workers in the cooperative here labour for three times the minimum wage beneath a portrait of Joseph Stalin. In the streets, posters for

LAURA'S TIPS: Women alone — staying safe

Whatever your age it is wise to take extra precautions against the small possibility of hassle or even attack:

✓ Dress like local women to avoid cultural misunder-standings. Cover up in baggy trousers or skirts and headscarves.

✓ Plan to arrive in daylight and pre-book your first night's accommodation.

✓ Check out destinations using web boards and guide books. If in doubt, stick to areas where you can meet up with other travellers.

✓ If a situation leaves you uncomfortable, walk away confidently towards a police station, busy shop or other women.

✓ If attacked, hand over your valuables. In desperate situations scream loudly and attack vulnerable parts (eyes, Adam's apple and groin) with your nails or a hard object like a key or pen.

✓ Always leave details of where you are going at your hostel.

✓ A few hours of self-defence training will boost both your self-awareness and confidence.

✓ Never drink alone in a bar or take drugs or sleep in public areas.

circuses compete with scarlet hammers and sickles and lurid images of Che Guevara.

Ten minutes later I'm in a world apart from all the communist graffiti, at the tiny village of Chirakkadavu as the temple drums announce a Theyyam ritual. I'm here at this village temple to watch a male priest turn into a goddess. The saffron and gold painted male dancer swirls his red skirts and tosses his headdress with its trailing black wig. To a crescendo of drums he descends to the sea and dips his bell-strung sword at the water's edge. Now the dance gets faster, horns blow and the bells on the dancer's feet and clothes jangle hypnotically as the priest's eyes grow fixed and remote. We leave as the villagers form an orderly queue to consult the 'goddess' about their worries. Transvestitism, communism, mysticism – Kerala is a colourful clash of ideas and faiths.

Day 20 Tellicherry, India

Tellicherry on the Keralan coast was for centuries a centre of the spice trade. It's here I get a break from eating to actually cook some food. Ayisha Manzil is a world-renowned homestay that offers cookery courses in Muslim-style Mapillah cuisine. Faiza Moosa is my tutor as we meet to prepare the night's feast – tamarind prawns, beef fry, vegetables stewed in coconut milk, chappathi and ghee rice.

The ingredients are beautifully prepared in tiny dishes: ochre and yellow dried spices plus tamarind, fresh coriander and curry leaves. My first surprise is that Faiza uses pressure cookers, saying they cook the food quickly before leaving it to mingle and mellow. My biggest challenge is making chappathi on a floured board and griddle. I go all fingers and thumbs as I try to fold my nice round chappathi into complicated square parcels. I feel sympathy for every Indian daughter learning to cook under a strict maternal eye.

Don't Indian men cook? I ask. No, no, Faiza assures me, only women – or the top chefs in hotels. I tell her about my husband's top dhals and that we share the cooking at home. Why ration the pleasure of cookery? But the pleasure is all ours as she serves the feast to me and my fellow guests, Chris and Janet. Richly flavoured, delicately balanced, the Tellicherry spice tradition still beats any British Indian restaurant.

Janet is researching her family history and trying to locate places from her grandfather's time in the Raj. She has already found a street where he lived and a few sites detailed in letters in photographs. 'But I wish I'd talked to more of the family before they died,' she says wistfully. I'm fascinated as I'm about to start my own family research in Indonesia next week. I've packed lots of notes and photos too, to try and find places where my ancestors lived more than a century ago.

Day 21 Pamba River, India

At my new homestay on the Pamba Backwaters my stomach has finally rebelled. I'm seeping onion and garlic from my pores now and just can't face my breakfast of bony fish and two hard-boiled eggs in green curry sauce. As I politely nibble the fish, the family mill around, staring and asking questions. Munching on a mouthful of fishbones I have to perform the difficult operation of sliding a bone out of my skewered tongue while continuing to explain for the hundredth time that my husband is working but will join me later. My homestay surroundings are extraordinary: a cut-out of Mother Teresa stares down from the wall beside an embroidered Christ with a sacred heart decorated with both red fairy lights and a live crawling lizard. But the conversation is warm and illuminating.

Chatting to Anjali, the educated young daughter of my homestay owner, she confides her problems with her Tamil maid. She is carefully saving the girl's salary for her to buy gold, she says. Remembering the endless advertisements I've seen of women weighed down in gold jewellery from headdresses to nose chains, I ask her why. 'Her parents take all her pay,' she explains. 'Without gold her parents will marry her off to an old drunkard who will beat her.'

It is my last day in Kerala so I go out on the backwaters. From a boat the river has a magical quality – at the water's edge villagers wash themselves, their clothes and brass pots, while thin black canoes slink silently beneath the waving palms and children paddle to school in criss-crossing boats. As the sun sets, lamps glow from modest houses and a storm growls and flickers across the *padi* fields.

Clambering off the boat to visit my boatman's home – thunk! Something hits my head in the dark. Ah, a tree helpfully growing in the middle of my pitch-dark path. I get the usual Indian questions: how many children? Do I work? How old am I? Everyone is so interested and friendly that it makes me realise how ungenerous with our time we have become in Britain. Wet from the storm and itchy from the bites I've endured in the service of politeness, I get back home to my unique outdoor shower. Only now I've got all the cold rain from the roof falling over me too and the pebble floor is agony on my feet. Scrambling out, I bang my head on the unhelpfully head-height soap dish. Lovely. A bruise on a bruise. Legs covered in red polka dots from standing chatting in the mosquito thick rain. Suddenly I've experienced enough of this watery world. Travelling alone has been so intense – full of remarkable people and wonder and strangeness – but there have also been the small annoyances and endless little niggles that I would have laughed off with a friend. I also confess I'm getting tired of electricity blackouts and no hot water or even no water at all. My most useful items so far have been my universal sink plug (used almost daily) and head-torch (used almost nightly to read in bed). I'm getting emails now from my sisters flying out from the UK and my son travelling in the opposite direction from New Zealand. Miraculously, we should all converge in Jakarta in 24 hours. Tomorrow I leave for hot volcanic Indonesia and I'm beginning to count down the hours.

THE FACTS: Keeping in touch

You will want to keep in touch with friends and family at home and contact people at your next destination, so try out different methods on the road:

- **Email** – cheap and available at hostels, hotels and internet cafes almost everywhere. Register a travelling address with Hotmail or Yahoo! for ease of access.

- **Phone cards** – make cheap phone calls via international calling cards available from local shops. They carry a freephone number that connects you to a cheap provider.

- **Phone offices** – make cheap phone calls where the locals go – a phone booth or office that charges by the minute.

- **Mobile phones** – great for emergencies, good for SMS but terrible for your budget. Speak to your provider about your plans before you leave. Consider buying a new SIM card abroad or even renting a new mobile.

- **Personal Digital Assistants (PDAs)** – need regular charging and a target for thieves. Great for journal writing and emailing on the road.

- A useful guide to all things electrical can be found at Steve Kropla's Help for World Travellers (www.kropla.com).

Travelling with others

Travelling with a companion or two has much obvious appeal. It feels safer, appears more sociable and feels far less scary. But whether you choose to fly off with a friend, a partner or family members, there are certain considerations to make about who travels with you. Before you rashly invite that old schoolfriend along, or a new mate from an internet bulletin board, it pays to think hard about compatibility.

One fundamental issue is budget. If you have always dreamed of splurging your way across the spas of Asia and your companion is hoping to find the cheapest hostel in Bangkok, you will have problems. Differences in both age and interests can upset even such naturally close companions as a mother and son. In Singapore Joanne was interested in culture and sightseeing while her 29-year old-son George mostly had one testosterone-fuelled interest – meeting girls:

'There was some friction. George was chatting up girls and leaving me behind like a spare part. The younger crowd got on my nerves sometimes but I was always glad I wasn't alone. Overall, we got on really well, supported each other and he put up with my moodiness.'

George agreed that despite the surface tensions, their relationship was strong enough to survive and deepen throughout the trip:

'Initially we had trouble adjusting to sharing our space together. It did become easier as the trip progressed. Both of you do need to have similar travelling interests to share the great moments (and sometimes the despair) together. Having said that, I would have made more friends if I had travelled alone. And you do need to wander off on your own and have some space at times.'

It can be difficult to predict just how a friendship that flourishes in the UK will be affected by the strains and struggles of travel. Over a few months you will see the best and worst of your companion. You will undoubtedly have to deal with that person's moods as they experience exhaustion and occasional tempers and sickness.

LAURA'S TIPS: Choosing a travel companion

Going off on a long trip with someone you don't know too well has been compared to getting married after a blind date. Not recommended. Think about the following points before booking twin rooms around the globe:

✓ Budget is crucial. Try to find someone with similar views on spending.

✓ Compatible goals. Do you want to see every sight in the guide book while they are looking to prop up the bar or find romance?

✓ Fitness. If your friend has health problems this may seriously compromise what you can achieve in those dream destinations.

✓ Take a trial trip together. A short holiday will soon reveal any problems.

✓ Build in time apart. Even the best of friends will enjoy a few weeks doing courses or tours in different company.

There is no doubt that choosing the wrong person to travel with could mean you pack your own personal nightmare. Susan learned that living 24 hours a day with a friend is quite different from seeing the same person in stress-free small doses. Unwilling to wait until her husband retired, she set off alone to meet up with various relatives and friends in Australia, Tasmania and New Zealand. Two friends she travelled with tested her patience:

> 'With two friends I had to bite my tongue and be very patient. I really wished I'd known before I set off that one of my travel companions was a control freak and the other one was interested only in herself. I know that sounds bitter but you live and learn. The whole thing also taught me things about myself.'

Travelling with your partner

For some travellers the idea of a long journey has been a shared dream for many years. It simply isn't an issue whether to travel together or not – it's a life-enriching experience intended to be shared and remembered together. Travelling as a couple can mean the extra security of two heads to work together on itineraries and to guard against scams. It's also usually cheaper as you can share a room and transport. But just like less committed travel companions, couples can also be apprehensive that the strain of travel may reveal fractures in their relationship. Jean, 61, joked about her worries when embarking on a winter's cricket tour of South America:

> 'I went with my husband Barry. We did wonder how we would get on for so long, travelling together. Would we kill each other? No, we got on as well as we do at home, where we spend some time together and some time on our own activities.'

Elize and Charles, on the other hand, had made an informal pact before setting off, that they would make an effort to work together whatever the crisis:

'*We agreed that if something went wrong, we had to stick together rather than fly off the handle. It can be dangerous to storm off on your own in a foreign city. When crises happened, like not being met off the train at Agra, we were surrounded by a crowd of about 30 people giving out lots of suspect advice. That was the good thing about the two of us travelling together, that I could go off and check things out while Charles looked after the luggage. You really have to keep your cool and operate as a team.*'

Michael also stressed the positive aspects of travelling with his fiancée, Mary-Ann:

'*Two heads are better than one when making a decision. And for the highpoints, a beautiful sunset is much nicer to share with someone than snapping it on a camera on your own.*'

Sharing the sheer boredom of travel without bickering is as much a test as working together in a crisis. Linda and James found that living their dream of travelling around the world for seven months strengthened their relationship:

'*Most of the time we were on our own. We really enjoyed each other's company – even the eight-hour drives across Australia with no change of scenery and no radio. It was a great way to strengthen our marriage.*'

Linda and James had not been married for long. What about older couples? Is it really possible to enjoy each other's company after decades of marriage? The last word goes to Gilly, 64:

'*As Ken works away for most weekdays, this was the first time we had spent week after week continually together – bliss!*'

Day 22 Colombo, Sri Lanka

I'm en route to Indonesia via Colombo and have a few hours' rest in the airport to check my email. My PDA has been my lifeline over the last few weeks, relaying texts and emails all without having to leave my room. First, the good news. My mum is happy and Yvonne has been taking her out for lots of treats. Next, my son is already waiting in Jakarta and reports that he's been out shopping in the sweltering heat. Not so good is the fact that Jakarta is crowded with protestors awaiting the imminent arrival of US President George Bush. I make a mental note to stay as far from potentially anti-western crowds as I can.

More worrying is the news from my husband Laurence. His dad has come out of hospital and Laurence is frantically trying to sort out food deliveries and set up home carers to visit him. He tells me he misses me and signs off 'deepest love'. I feel the insistent tug of guilt and tears come to my eyes knowing that there is nothing I can do to help them all back at home.

Day 23 Jakarta, Java, Indonesia

Meeting my son, Chris, and sisters Marijke and Lorraine in Indonesia gives me a huge high as we hug each other with pure happiness. Travelling alone was intense and extra vivid but always carried an edge of anxiety that I can now leave behind for a while. For days we gather in emotional huddles to recount adventures, giggle like teenagers and cry as we remember our father's recent death and mum's current illness. The hotel staff must think we are crazy as we veer from laughing like chimps to sobbing hysterically every few minutes.

At last we can carry out our plan to explore our family's heritage on the island of Java, where our mother was born, and investigate our Dutch ancestors. We've brought photographs, information and addresses and are ready to hit the trail. More than 70 years after my family fled Java as the Second World War approached, will there be any traces left of their life on Java? With our excellent tour guide Imam and driver Donno, we leave smoggy Jakarta and George Bush behind as fast as we can and hit the open road to traverse Java from the west to east coast.

Day 25 Cirebon, Java, Indonesia

We're in search of a palace with blue Delft tiles. One of our more interesting ancestors was Elizabeth Petronella Heidenreich, born 1855, the daughter of a German officer and a Javanese princess. My mother knew her as a regal old lady who continued to bear the royal title 'Gusti'. She had spoken of her childhood in Cirebon where she played in a palace room with chandeliers and Dutch tiles.

These days Cirebon is a hectic but friendly city, famous for its prawns and a lively market like a medieval encampment amidst heaps of exotic fruits, cloths and spices. However, there are two palaces in Cirebon since the royal family split in the 16th century. We begin our inquiries at the older Kesapuhan palace where the Sultana herself, Ratu Dalem Hj Sri Mulya, the present Sultan's mother, kindly answers our questions on the family's history. She is a gracious and fine-boned lady no taller than our shoulders who offers us drinks on a French-style sofa on her marble open-air veranda. We learn that the Muslim sultans had many wives – and, of course, many children including daughters who were known as Princess or 'Gusti'. Inside the palace is a room with a few Delft tiles and we wonder if we have reached our goal. The palace also contains many wonderful objects of strangely hybrid Hindu, Chinese and Arabian style: a dragon-winged chariot, ceremonial masks, puppets and weaponry, alongside tarnished chandeliers and mirrors reminiscent of Versailles. Back in the time of our great great grandmother, Java's importance as a spice producer meant that many small sultanates traded with the west and imitated the courts of Europe.

Then we visit the second palace of Kanoman. Here the Sultan looks at our papers and through a messenger reports that Heidenreich met Elizabeth's mother after calling at the palace to conduct trade. And at this palace we strike gold: an audience chamber and throne room encrusted with ancient Delft tiles. This is undoubtedly where my great great grandmother played as a child. I touch the beautiful unfaded tile, a valuable gift to the royal family from Europe, and feel I touch a little piece of my own personal history.

Day 27 Wonosobo, Java, Indonesia

It is my son Chris's birthday and we are at Wonosobo, the gateway to the mysterious Dieng plateau called Di-Hyang, the Abode of the Gods. Here we are the only tourists viewing some of the most ancient Hindu temples in Java, lost in swamps for many years and rediscovered in 1814. We are staying at the beautifully restored Hotel Kresna when our guide, Imam, calls Chris to meet him alone before dinner. None of us suspects what he has in mind.

As we sip our cocktails the figure of a sultan approaches in glittering waistcoat and feathered turban. He's being bowed to and applauded by the hotel staff – and then we see it's Chris! It's a great laugh to see him in his finery and we learn that this is a common way to celebrate special occasions on Java. But despite the costume he has not quite achieved the divine status awarded him on the hotel staff's birthday card: 'Happy Aniversary', it reads, 'for Mr Christ'.

Day 28 Wonosobo, Java, Indonesia

Behind the armies of scooters, traffic noise and swarming crowds it is still possible to glimpse old Java in the countryside. Outside the cities, the rice and vegetable terraces soar high towards the volcanic peaks, and workers in the fields labour as they have done for centuries, mostly with their hands, and an occasional pair of water buffalo. Old folk still dress in layers of batik, babies are tied to working women's backs and triangular coolie hats shade them from the sun. Yet undoubtedly Java is changing: many young women wear western clothes with an Islamic headscarf, use mobile phones and aspire to drive the people carriers that clog the roads. Gentle gamelan gongs clash with the muezzin's call to prayer but it is the traffic noise that finally wins. Indonesia is the fourth largest country in the world and it is changing fast.

Day 29 Jogjakarta, Java, Indonesia

Approaching Borobudur, the eighth-century Budhhist temple abandoned for a thousand years and then rediscovered in the jungle, we are almost mobbed. But the crowds are Indonesian youngsters on school trips clamouring to talk to or be photographed with us big white native English speakers. Western travellers are a rarity on Java since all the big tour operators dropped Indonesia as a destination. To cries of 'Miss, Miss!' and 'Where you from?' we let them include us in their photos as they whoop and giggle. One man even puts up a tripod, sets the timer and strolls casually over to stand close beside me and pose sheepishly as his camera clicks.

Then, from the lowest tier representing the real world to the crowning summit 34m higher, we climb to nirvana between Buddhas and stunning carvings telling the tale of Siddhartha. As we leave, high school students clamour around us, eager to record an interview for their English project. 'Why are you here?' and 'What music do you like?' they ask, before repeatedly inquiring, 'Aren't you frightened of terrorists?' They know the reason they rarely see western tourists any more. The majority of Indonesians are polite, happy, exuberant – even enlightened – but cursed by a tiny minority casting a shadow across their nation.

Day 31 Malang, Java, Indonesia

Equipped with an address and old photographs from the 1920s, we arrive in Malang, east Java. It's the town where my Dutch mother had an idyllic childhood, living in her grandparents' house across the road from a stylish outdoor swimming pool. The photos we have show orderly white Dutch buildings and empty roads. Arriving at night after a 10-hour drive there is little to recognise amongst the electronic stores, mosques and street vendors.

Next day we cruise along the chaotic street and find the address. At first all we can see is a huge signboard for a college. Inside, the house has been partitioned into tiny classrooms crowded with chairs and whiteboards. Yet we can just discern the shell of the old colonial building among the floor tiles and high, corniced ceilings. In a store at the back of the courtyard we even find the original leaded front doors from our old photographs – kept, we are told, because such salvage can be valuable. I find the few old rooms where my mum used to stay, now painted garish red for luck by a former Chinese occupant. Old cupboards, doors and shutters still remain and hot tears rise as I surrender to the atmosphere of this place where my mum spent some of the happiest years of her life. Through my teary eyes I can almost feel her girlhood presence – carefree and loved – playing out in the shady courtyard.

Day 34 Malang, Java, Indonesia

I'm enjoying the ambience of the gorgeous Tugu Hotel in Malang, part antiques museum, part Disneyesque luxury experience. A manager takes us on the hotel tour to see Arabian suites with multicoloured gossamer drapes, beds as big as rooms and private tented spas. There are restaurants at the end of avenues of palm trees, Chinese meeting halls and lanterns and candles everywhere creating a wild, romantic atmosphere. Also here is the Tugu Teahouse with its range of exotic Indonesian sweetmeats served each afternoon. Morsels of coconut pancakes, sweet spring rolls and steamed nuts and fruits cooked in banana leaves keep alive the old traditions. The Tugu takes the best of the old east and gives it a modern, madly romantic western twist.

It's time to say our goodbyes now – one sister, Lorraine, is flying back to the UK and Chris is returning to New Zealand. It's been a wonderful achievement finally to visit this steamy volcanic island, teeming with young people and yet still redolent of the romance of the old East Indies. I feel energised and inspired, and also very happy that this experience was shared. As my son Chris says, 'I'm so glad I shared this trip. Otherwise all our family history would soon be forgotten.' He's only sorry that work will keep him from our next destination – Flores, a mysterious lost world of dragons and evolutionary quirks that promises to be a world away from the gentle sophistication of east Java.

THE POINT OF IT ALL

Day 34 Rinca, Indonesia

'I am sorry to tell you,' our new guide Mr Piter tells us, 'but women who are menstruating are forbidden to visit Komodo National Park. The male dragons can smell the blood from 5km.' No need to worry, we say, unable to stop giggling. 'And they've got two penises,' my sister Marijke whispers. 'I don't want one of those after me!'

I've flown to Flores with Marijke and a new arrival from London, her husband David. David is a big, jovial guy of 58 while Marijke is an elegant former airline worker in her mid-50s. I'm concerned that Flores might be a bit too rough for them but they just laugh it off. Hmm, let's wait and see, I think. Flores is about two hours by air east of Java along a glorious archipelago of tiny islands. The lush volcanic island is barely touched by tourism and during our week we see only a couple of other young Europeans, also with local guides. Our first priorities are the giant monitor lizards known as Komodo Dragons and next morning we're off on a boat from the charmingly ramshackle harbour of Labuanbajo. Our destination is rocky Rinca, an island we're told supports far more dragons than the more famous Komodo island.

Before we set sail a young man shows us a scar on his leg from a lizard that found him napping. 'One month in hospital,' he beams. He's lucky – a tourist bitten in 2001 died from the poisonous bacteria found lurking in Komodo saliva. There are older accounts of humans beings maimed and eaten by these throwbacks to dinosaurs.

It's a blissful three-hour trip between the volcanic cones of dozens of sunlit islands. The sun is sparkling on the treacherous deep blue waters as I listen to the perfect audio book written exactly on this spot: David Attenborough's *Zoo Quest for a Dragon* (BBC Audiobooks 2006). As we disembark at the tiny jetty one of our teenage sailors pokes beneath the platform with a forked stick. A perfectly camouflaged 4ft dragon slithers out and begins to eye up a monkey which crouches foolishly near. We creep past and with a trained ranger make a start on a 5km trek that proves gruelling in the 38°C heat.

There are plenty of dragons: babies, slothful males and a lively female digging her nest. Protected by men with sticks, we can explore Rinca's barren landscape of eerie dead swamps and dried out river beds. Today the giant lizards are mostly sleepy as they waddle through the dust or eye us languidly with beadlike eyes. They will feed later, the ranger tells us. By then we're glad to be away across the water, snorkelling on a stunning reef. But still Marijke won't clamber down the wooden ladder from the boat into the water. She's seen a documentary about Komodo dragons that can swim. Even as I explore the rainbow corals I can't help shooting the odd glance behind my back – I don't fancy becoming dragon dinner just yet.

Day 37 Liangbua, Flores, Indonesia

Since news was first announced of the so-called 'Hobbit People' – 8,500-year-old fossils of 3ft-tall Homo floresiensis – I've been fascinated to find out more. Flores is not only a wildly beautiful island but an ecological puzzle. Animals have evolved to unusual sizes: tiny elephants, giant rats, colossal lizards and, now, the tiniest humans ever recorded.

Our first trip to a cave at Batu Cermin had been a surprising insight into this 'soft adventure' tour. It was very, very hot as we tramped up the road towards a massive cliff like the volcanic plateau in the movie *King Kong*. At least it will be cool inside, we gasped. Then the scrambling started. I picked my way up the boulders, Marijke more cautious behind me and David, agile but puffing, brought up the rear. After a lot of squeezing through passages we suddenly find there's only one way out – it's about 3ft high, the size of a small fireplace and jagged with stalactites. The petite Indonesian guide slips through and then it's our turn. 'Oh, God,' my sister groans, shuffling down onto all fours. I wince to see her M&S trousers and spotless white T-shirt caked with brown dust. 'I forgot to tell them Fat Boy was coming,' pants David, eyeing the tiny entrance. With much puffing he squeezes through and emerges breathless at the other end of a tunnel. We are standing in a large but airless chamber. 'Look at the part Sure deodorant didn't work on,' announces David, mimicking the advert. Every part of his shirt is soaked in sweat. Above us hangs a bat, thankfully in some kind of hibernation, beside spiders the size of tea plates. Then the crawling starts again. I can't stop giggling. It's like the horror movie *The Descent* – if this is the 'soft' adventure how hard is the hard stuff going to be?

I ask Marijke and David if they want to see the 'Hobbit' cave next and gamely they say they do. After a bone-rattling ride in a specially chartered van, we arrive at remote Liang Bua cave where curious locals and the cave's officer-in-charge gather to show us round. This cave is a beautiful, natural arch leading into the mountainside, offering a natural well and numerous hiding holes and niches. Augustus, a young man who helped on the historic dig, shows us where the controversial female skull was found alongside a tiny elephant.

High up on the wall is the hole identified as the 3ft high people's sleeping chamber. 'Too difficult for you,' our guide says. 'You're too old.' Too old? I decide to have a go and clamber up the well-worn footholds in the boulder wall. Then I see a low opening overhung by stalactites. I'm almost twice the little people's height but somehow I squeeze through and emerge into a tall chamber beautifully rippled with pearly rock formations. The officer points out another small hole formerly used as an exit but 'too small for us'.

I'm awed to have visited this site, guessing that soon the sleeping chamber will be off limits to tourists like me. For centuries local legends survived of a race of little people who once lived in the forest – now science can at last prove them true.

Travellers' highlights

It can be a risky question, asking a newly returned gapper to describe the highlights of their trip. You may still be listening three hours later with mouth open and brain numbed at the sheer variety of wonderful moments recalled. And you may also be starting to wonder, could I do this? Travel is infectious and all great travellers' tales raise a challenge. Where would you go? And what would you do? And what exactly is holding you back?

Physical challenge

Our grown-up travellers' highlights follow a couple of striking themes. Challenge is the first. Doing something completely new that confronts your own ideas about yourself can be a thrilling activity.

Despite having survived a stroke, 53-year-old Polly had been drawn to making a parachute jump for a long time. She got her chance in South Africa after meeting a tandem partner she described as 'a six-foot-three drop-dead gorgeous hunk called Jimbob' in a bar:

> 'We flew for 30 minutes over the coast and my nerves diminished as we flew low over schools of dolphin, hammerhead sharks and whales. The view was spectacular. We climbed to 10,000ft and I received a gentle kiss on the cheek as my safety straps were tightened in preparation. There is a little step outside the plane and I was told to put my feet on it and cross my arms over my body. Suddenly I was gone . . . Jimbob and I somersaulted out of the plane and we were flying, we were in freefall plummeting at 125 miles an hour, but it didn't feel like that, it was slow and quiet and I felt I was in heaven. Jimbob was right, it was the best experience of my life.'

Achieving something that physically scares you creates a massive boost to self-confidence. No longer are skydiving and bungee jumping the preserve of the young backpacker – lots of mature gappers are getting in on the act. On reaching New Zealand's adrenaline centre of Rotorua, James and Linda literally plunged straight in at the deep end:

> 'We chose to go white-water rafting and thought we would start at the beginning (not) and found a grade five river classed as "extreme". We did a 7m drop (in a 4m dinghy) and survived, and several other smaller drops. Thankfully, the boat did not overturn. So we thought we would then try sledging the rest of the river, imagining this to be a gentle ride holding on to the sledge, which is like a buoyancy aid with handles. How wrong we were. We were plunging down 3m drops into icy cold water and then turning around as if in a wash cycle, before surfacing, gasping for breath, as the instructor shouted at us to swim 'turbo' speed across the

raging river. Not quite the thing for two unfit people who can barely swim, and should have seriously run more, smoked less and not had a bottle or two of wine last night. We survived though, this time without the energy to walk!'

Kate was less adventurous than her action man husband Keith who happily disappeared into jungles to kayak, bushwalk and what Kate described as 'play at being Ray Mears'. But in Australia a bush camping trip proved to be a surprise highlight:

'I have never felt so dirty in my life but had a wonderful time. We went swimming in the most wonderful places and climbed Jim Jim Falls which was magnificent. It was very challenging but a total highlight.'

Susan also learned that she was less physically limited at the age of 60 than she had anticipated. She conquered a whole series of fears and firsts:

'After being scared of heights, I climbed Sydney Harbour Bridge even with trains, cars and boats far beneath my feet. I also learned to fish for the first time and immediately caught a fish and then ate it. I also learned to sail and rode a quad bike for the first time.'

Sue got the chance to share all this fun with her two young sons and plant the seed of wanderlust in their hearts too. Faced with the kinds of experiences they could not find in the UK, Sue's own pleasure was richly amplified:

'I have brilliant lifelong memories of seeing my children experience so many brilliant things. They scuba dived on the Great Barrier Reef, camped in the Daintree Rainforest, sand surfed in New Zealand, experienced the wonder of Waitomo, saw many Maori cultural events, experienced rock climbing, white-water rafting, the list goes on . . .'

Meeting people

The chance to meet different and fascinating people is another highlight recounted by travellers. Meeting local people and learning about their lives is a key element of the allure of exotic travel. Even though Tim's goal was to spend time alone, he found the mix of new landscapes and people he met on the road exhilarating:

> 'There were so many highs it would be impossible to pick any one out. The mountain roads to Marrakesh, the unexpected "wow" moments as one rounded a bend or crested a hill, waking up to the sun and the sound of the ocean after my first night in Morocco, the people, Christmas and New Year, the sheep festival, Mohammed Oumolou, meeting Zahira, Tafroute, Sidi Aglou, weddings, dancing, singing, laughing, losing two stone, feeling so young . . . sorry, I am getting carried away. I had a five-month highlight!'

Emrys admits that as a volunteer in Africa you will always be perceived as a westerner simply because you can choose to go home:

> 'But that's not to say that you can't integrate into the community and be invited to weddings and funerals, go down to the pub and watch a football match. Watching Cameroon play football in the World Cup (and I hate football) in a tiny little room with a black and white television run off a car battery with all these people who are so excited that there's a black team winning a football match – that was something else.'

Polly's mix of travelling and volunteering in South Africa made it simple for her to describe the highlights:

> 'My high points are always the people one meets along the way. I aim to learn about myself and others.'

Gilly also singled out the people she met:

'My highlight was meeting amazing people. The spiritual environment of a four-hour walk at twilight in Waipoua Forest with two Maori guides. At each place I chose to stay there was a connection with the people we met in terms of interests of spiritually.'

Working in Australia after his mother Joanne had gone home meant that George came into contact with more varied people than he would have on the hostel circuit. Having a working visa brought him experiences he could never have obtained in the UK:

'I worked with famous athletes at the Commonwealth Games. I saw the highs (celebrations with medals and access to big sporting events) and also the lows (syringes left beside beds – and tantrums). Next, I worked at the Korean Bath House in Kings Cross, Sydney. There was an amazing mix of clients from famous actors and business owners to contact with prostitutes and members of the seedy underworld. Experiences like those make you wake up to what the world's about and give you a stock of incredible memories.'

The chance to share and connect with others and have your mind truly broadened is summarised by Paul:

'For me the greatest outcome was meeting lots of people from around the world and sharing different ideas and views.'

There is also a rejuvenating effect when moving amongst younger travellers. 70-year-old Fran found that younger backpackers were far friendlier than the older, more affluent travellers she met. One highlight for her was joining up with some younger people for part of her New Zealand leg:

'I travelled for four days with a 40-year-old guy and a couple of 27-year-olds. They were in a campervan and we went all round the Caitlins together. It was very unspoilt, had wonderful wildlife and there were fascinating places like a petrified forest. It was

mind-blowing. My son said my itinerary was as hectic as an 18–30 holiday. But I did say that the difference is I'll be going to bed on my own and sober. Well, in the event not always sober. One night we went out for dinner and then on to a pub. And John, a young American guy, walked me home at quarter past two in the morning!'

Discovering landscapes and cultures

Unsurprisingly, the natural and cultural wonders of the world feature strongly in travellers' memories. By taking a long trip, gap travellers have unhurried time to take in great cities, landscapes and natural wonders at their leisure.

Abby's rail odyssey to eastern Europe brought her into areas far away from commercial tourism. Travelling alone, her highlights were the unique cultures she had access to:

'I loved the excitement of arriving in a new country and exploring the wonders of each city. I'd set off early in the morning with my guide book and a full day of discovery ahead of me. One Czech family I stayed with even took me up to their chalet in the mountains. We visited beautiful Konopiste Castle and the lost villages of the area, all untouched by tourism.'

For Josh it was his long-awaited trip to Japan:

'What an amazing culture Japan has – all polite manners, rituals, sushi trains and bowing elevator assistants. My highlights are a magical sight of Mount Fuji, and the Shizuoka prefecture, one of the most beautiful parts of Japan. I also loved historic Kyoto, especially wandering at night through small twisting back alleys where lanterns glow outside steamy noodle bars. I also got to central Tokyo and saw all the TV screens on buildings, neon flashing and party people filling the streets.'

Natural wonders like the Great Barrier Reef also rate highly in travellers' memories. Sometimes everything comes together – the tour, weather and the sights – as Kate and Keith found:

> 'For us it was Australia and the Whitsunday Island trip in particular. We booked a two-day cruise on an old sailing ship to the Great Barrier Reef – it was absolutely magnificent! Nothing topped it. If anything, it spoiled us for everywhere else. I have never been anywhere so beautiful.'

Ajay visited Bagan in Burma after swapping emails with travel writer William Dalrymple who told him it was his favourite place on earth:

> 'I could not agree more. In 16 sq miles, approximately 2,500 pagodas and temples are scattered. We first went to see the beautiful Ywa Haung Gyi temple. We climbed to the top. The view from above was breathtaking. Look right, left, front, back, one sees only pagodas, stupas and temples, hundreds and thousands of them, of various size and shape, of architectural excellence – serene, sombre, each containing Buddha's statue.'

Reflection

'Time out from life,' 'a chance to reflect' and 'gaining a new perspective' are phrases used again and again to describe time spent away from the humdrum of life exploring other parts of the globe. Some of the travellers I meet are keen to discuss the idea of a 'golden' gap year as more than just a holiday. For them it's a chance to gain distance from daily concerns and reflect on life. As a rite of passage, the older person's gap year appears even more powerful than the traditional pre- or post-university gap. It is certainly a rebellion against all the stereotypes of old age as helpless or comfort-seeking. Instead it is a way of expressing freedom, extending youthfulness, connecting with nature and physical challenge.

Written journals

Keeping a record of the trip is an important part of the reflective experience. Keeping a journal is also a keystone of self-development, encouraging insights and new approaches. Psychological theory tells us that by reflecting on experiences in journal form we encourage new ways of thinking and positive learning. Rather than the 'seen it, done it' journals of their younger counterparts, many older travellers use the whole experience to question who they are and how they have lived their lives.

All the travellers I talked to kept some form of written record. Those with a partner at home or close family ties tended to send detailed emails that they then collected into a record of the trip. Joanne planned each email she wrote so that it could eventually be displayed with her photographs:

> 'My written journal was quite scrappy and tended to be full of calculations of different currencies and observations of people. But my emails to my boyfriend and family were the full record of my trip. I did a weekly email with headings "Best moment," "Worst moment," "Curious incidents," and so on. I tried to use all five senses to evoke the places. You can be overwhelmed with sensory detail on a trip and a weekly record helped me focus on what was different about what I was seeing, hearing, smelling and eating.'

Susan also used her regular emails to reflect in some depth and help other people at home share her trip:

> 'My diaries are in the form of 29 emails and are a day-to-day record for myself and those who wanted them. I've had some very good comments from people who enjoyed them. I mention observations on lifestyle, differences in culture, the weather and activities.'

The time to be creative allows lots of gappers to try out new means of expression. As well as keeping a journal and sending emails home, Sue wrote up the whole round the world trip for her and her sons:

> 'I wrote the whole thing up into a book at the end which amounted to about 120,000 words. Regretfully I never managed to get it published but it was fun writing it and helps us all to remember our experiences.'

But what if there is no email available? Emrys stayed in remote villages where even the radio telephone was only a means to contact the local missionary station. It forced him to write old-fashioned letters in such volume that he soon wryly realised they weren't always appreciated:

> 'Absolutely nothing happens after 6 o'clock at night when it gets dark so I had loads of time to write. But everyone else back in the UK is getting on with their own lives, saying "I've got another letter from Emrys today. Oh bugger, I've got nothing new to say." I did get the feeling that some people thought I was bugging them or something. So you don't continue to write to people if you don't get a reply. Because the reply is the important bit!'

As well as email, many travellers use technology to make a record of their travels and keep in touch with friends and family at home. Tim is posting a blog on the internet under the pseudonym 'Bill' as told by his teddy bear 'Ted':

> 'The chronicles of Bill as he goes through midlife, as told by his long-suffering bear, forced to go along with the plan to find all the answers in Morocco – and I don't even know the questions!' (www.billandtedsadventure.blogspot.com)

Also technically able, Paul used his skills to chronicle his travels:

> 'I put together a website and took heaps of pictures and wrote emails.'

For those not wanting to set up a website or blog, a simple alternative is to register with a travel website and post regular updates and photos. By filling in diary pages and attaching pictures, your travels can be shared not only by those you have left at home but also by the wider travelling community. Ajay, for example, documented his trip by using lots of different media:

'I took photographs, wrote a diary, made a video and wrote a journal on www.travellersconnected.com.'

As a memento of the trip, Gilly is keen to use her papercraft skills to make a creative scrapbook of words and images:

'I have photographs, video and a diary. I have the scrapbook and materials and now I'm about to start!'

Photography

A reliable camera is likely to be top of your packing list and these days it will probably be digital. Digital photography has a number of advantages over film including the sheer number of photographs that can be taken, instantly viewed and quickly deleted if they don't quite work. Digital photographs can also easily be attached to your emails, blog or online journal. The major disadvantage is the frequent need to charge your camera's battery. In many developing countries this may mean plugging into the mains at specific times before a blackout. Do check ahead if you are travelling into remote areas without electricity. In that case you will need to take a film camera and plenty of film.

Another potential difficulty with digital is getting all your digital images backed up and saved each time the camera's storage is full. It may be simple to get your photos stored on a CD in a busy tourist destination but much less straightforward in remote parts of the world. If in doubt, bring extra digital memory cards or storage media with you.

LAURA'S TIPS: Choosing a camera

✓ Pocket digital cameras are best for unobtrusive snaps. Even a good mobile phone camera can create good-quality candid images.

✓ For wildlife a good optical zoom is essential.

✓ Investigate the quality of the viewfinder and screen. Remember an LCD screen may not be as clear in bright sunshine.

✓ Try to test the camera for its ease of use.

✓ Digital SLRs (single lens reflex) will provide slightly better image quality but are bulkier, weightier and often need additional lenses.

✓ Consider your camera's full volume and weight including cables, chargers, adaptors, spare batteries and manual.

✓ Know your gear — spend a few months before departure testing night, action and macro (close-up) settings.

✓ Be vigilant — keep your camera charged up, clean and safe.

However careful you are with your camera bag and gear, things can go wrong. Cameras can develop faults so it is wise to pack a troubleshooting guide, your camera warranty and a list of authorised repairs centres. Over a time period like a year, travellers like Kate and Keith took more than 6,000 pictures but inevitably had minor accidents on the way:

'On the drive to Cooktown Keith decided to hang his camera up in the campervan then opened the window. He then decided to try my new hat on and elbowed his camera out the window. Doh! It bounced but survived – or so we thought. It then suffered from post traumatic stress syndrome. Keith will have to spend hours with Photoshop getting rid of dots.'

Sometimes, however much care you take or however good your camera is, even the process of getting your pictures saved on disc can go wrong. Fran was in New Zealand when a photography shop lost some of her images:

'Unfortunately when I had my photos put onto disc they missed out 30 photographs so I don't have proof of me sand boarding down the dunes at Cape Reinga. I deleted the memory card. I only took two with me. One was in the camera being used and when the other one was full I got it printed and deleted it.'

Day 39 Boloji, Flores, Indonesia

'After Africans, Indonesians are the world's most magic people,' our guide Piter tells me. Centuries of isolation have left Flores with unique tribal areas and customs. Villages of wooden houses with steep, slender thatched roofs cluster around ritual areas of miniature houses and carved male and female figures. In Boloji we are greeted by the whole village of Ngadha people streaming towards us in a Ja'i dance of greeting. Men in elaborate sarongs, sashes and belts lift their swords as they cry and stamp. The women are more

LAURA'S TIPS: Getting the best travel shots

✓ Try to capture the essence of a place. Is it serene, bustling, bleak or highly decorated?

✓ Go out in the early morning or late afternoon for the best light.

✓ Don't just take pictures — give them. Befriend your subjects and offer to post on prints.

✓ Walk around, look at angles and aim for a different approach to famous sights.

✓ Take 10 times the number of your usual shots to capture that one perfect moment.

✓ Learn how to use the remote-related feature to include yourself against vivid backgrounds.

✓ Fill the viewfinder with local signs, decorative architecture, graffiti and interesting foodstuffs.

✓ Use arches, walls and windows as frames.

✓ After asking permission, photograph people in action, working, resting and interacting.

soberly dressed in black woven ikat cloths and carry fur-trimmed shoulder bags, bead strings and headbands. They are a wonderfully welcoming group, entertaining us with their Suling bamboo orchestra, playing *Sayonara*, a relic of the unhappy invasion of Flores by the Japanese.

The women of the bamboo orchestra tell us through an interpreter that they have no photographs of themselves so we take lots of shots of them in their traditional dresses, smiling broadly to show red betel-nut stained teeth. Sitting on plastic chairs we are offered sweet tea and temporary tribe status by donning robes and head-bands. It could all feel a bit commercialised but it doesn't. We learn that Paul, the manager of our tour company, is the chief's brother and he has arranged this entertainment for his 'VIP' guests. It feels very natural and at the end of the dancing we are ushered away so the gathered tribe can get on with their private village meeting.

Later, in the Nagekeo village of Boawae I reach out to touch the rit-ual pole beside the shrunken-headed figure representing the vil-lage's potent male ancestor spirit. It's sticky and I wonder if it has been tarred. Just looking around me I should have guessed – each house is decorated with rows of animal skulls, preferably water buffalo, but at a cost of three million rupiah each (more than £150), pigs are often substituted. This ancient carved tree trunk transplanted from the forest by the tribe's ancestors is where the animals have their throats cut, our guide Piter cheerfully tells us.

Even Piter, though a Roman Catholic, seems to have a soft spot for ritual magic. As a child, he attended a rain-making ritual at which pigs and chickens were sacrificed beneath a sacred tree. 'A fog formed in the sky and soon it rained,' he insists. Only recently he asked a 'paranormal' woman to help him trace a lost mobile phone. After communication with his dead parents and an offer-ing of cigarettes at their grave the phone was mysteriously returned. 'And what about humans?' I ask uneasily. 'When did human sacrifice end?' 'Finally it was only slaves,' he assures me. 'So,' I ask, 'it ended when the Catholic missionaries came in the 19th century?' 'No, in the 1950s,' Piter replies. 'Human sacrifice was made against the law then.' Flores is isolated and utterly unique, I think. But I am glad I wasn't here 50 years ago.

Day 41 Moni, Flores, Indonesia

Flores has been a real insight into what makes a great adventure. Our days have been a wild succession of wonderful people and thrilling sights, all enhanced by lush tropical landscape surrounding soaring plateaus. But our nights have been, well – dire. The hotels have been so awful that despite our daily jokes about heading for 'The Shrunken Head Hotel' we've still been flabbergasted by how bad they've been. To describe just one: picture a building site of bamboo scaffolding and my incredulity as I'm led through a cacophony of laughing workmen, shrieking pigs and crowing cockerels to the most horrible room I could imagine. Above me in the room's roofspace I can hear yet more shuffling and banging. Is it birds, rats or something just too scary for my imagination to grasp? Outside my room are cupboard-style recesses with filthy mattresses and sleeping figures who might be staff but then again might not be, as there's no actual service at this hotel.

My big damp room is dominated by the most unpleasant ornament I've ever seen. It's a broken glass case containing a stuffed ant-eating bird (imagine a beak like two Kirby grips) attacking a stuffed snake. Intrigued, I see an antiquated light switch and realise the scene is supposed to be illuminated. Click. Unfortunately I disturb something that slithers quickly out of the base. I jump back. Next, I investigate the bathroom. A quick wash reveals some novel plumbing. When I remove my eternally useful sink plug, the water drains out of the stubby pipe – on to my feet. I later find that I'm lucky. My toilet actually flushes, unlike Marijke and David's. We just keep repeating our mantra – maybe tomorrow will be better. It never is.

When does this carefree mood change? Laurence sends me the news I have been dreading. His father has died peacefully in hospital, just 10 days before Laurence's flight to join me for Christmas in Sri Lanka. I am haunted by my last goodbye to my father-in-law, pale and weak in a hospital bed as I leaned to kiss his dry lips goodbye. Before I left I had agreed with Laurence that if the worst happened I wouldn't fly home for the funeral. Nevertheless, it's hard not to fantasise about flying home and supporting my husband at this sad time. After travelling for so long, I admit that there's also something tempting about going home for a week and letting the cool winter air refresh my humidity-addled brain and also (joy of joys) replacing my tattered wardrobe. Then my airline-savvy sister Marijke bursts my bubble. Apparently, it would be impossible to get new flights back out to New Zealand during the busy Christmas season.

Day 45 Kelimutu, Flores, Indonesia

Today my PDA relays a message from Laurence that his father's funeral has been arranged for 17 December – just four days before his flight out to Sri Lanka. I will be able to attend a second ceremony to inter my father-in-law's ashes when I return home in the New Year.

It has been a disturbing day. We got up at dawn to visit the famous Three-Coloured Lakes of Kelimutu. These are the lakes of the dead where the Floressans believe the people's '*mutu*' or spirits rest. We tramp up an eerily silent volcano where three great craters contain motionless lakes of impenetrable, mineral-rich water. Once red, white and blue, the lakes gradually change colour according to mineral levels. In what is today a greenish lake, lie the souls of children. In the brown lake are the elderly, while evil-doers are consigned to the black lake. It seems fitting to be standing here in this unearthly place of barren rock where for centuries the dead have been remembered. I feel worlds away from Britain and its pre-Christmas shopping frenzy. It would seem fitting to throw an offering into the lake but Piter makes it clear this is no comforting memorial. Only last year, he tells us, a pair of Dutch tourists climbed up on the crater rim, slipped into the water and were never found. The smooth inner surface of the crater would offer no purchase, and besides, the poisonous water would kill anything that fell inside. In Floressan mythology the *mutu* spirits are at their strongest here and I stand a long time in the chilly dawn, simply remembering the dead.

WHEN THINGS GO WRONG

Day 49 Galle, Sri Lanka

Until the news of my father-in-law's death it had all been going so well. From Kenya to Flores everything had gone better than I could have wished for. I'd seen incredible sights far beyond my expectations and met fascinating people of so many races and religions. Suddenly the atmosphere changed. Maybe I got travel weary or maybe good times never last.

Still with Marjike and David, I'd had a few days downtime in Ubud, Bali – perfect time to relax in the exotic oasis of the Alam Shanti Hotel. But I'd caught a cold and was feeling tired and run down. Or maybe it was that final therapeutic massage that reduced my pummelled limbs to jelly. Advertised as sorting out my *chakras*, I read in the salon leaflet that if my chakras 'does not werk well, it will be a negative efeck in the serrounding organs'. The 'efecks' of healing are not too inspiring: '1. Oftem yawns because the energy goes out through the mouth. 2. Can make asleep because our body needs a rest.' Too true – I'm totally shattered. As for the third and final 'efeck' – 'Some time the patient wants to take a pis.' Not quite the enticing promotional literature we've grown to expect from Champneys and the like.

I wasn't looking forward to the long flight alone via Kuala Lumpur back to Sri Lanka. Packing my daysack for a night in Kuala Lumpur's transit hotel I crammed in my nightwear, fresh clothes, PDA, toiletries and documents – all the rest had to go in my case. Alarm bells sounded when the airline refused to check my bag through to Sri Lanka, quoting security issues. That left me with a problem. I had pre-booked into the airside hotel and couldn't cross customs where my bag needed to be claimed. Reluctantly, I agreed to follow Malaysian airline's instructions and allow it to be kept in the airline's store overnight. Anxiety about losing my bag kept me sleepless most of the night so it was with great relief that I finally saw my bag out alone on the tarmac ready to load on my final Colombo-bound flight. When I picked it up in Sri Lanka I thought all was well.

Next day in rainy Galle I noticed a strange security tag around the double padlocks that lock my case. My case had been tampered with and a variety of items stolen. The worst – the most sickening – was my lovely pocket digital camera, along with all my photos so far. And yes, I'd broken every sensible rule and not backed my pictures up. All my fantastic, unique photos and video clips had been stolen, undoubtedly by an airline employee. It was hard to explain to my homestay host what had happened as tears choked my voice, prompted both by rage at someone tampering with my case and terrible sadness at the loss of this unique record of my trip.

Dealing with problems

The good news is that the majority of travellers never encounter any serious difficulties or dangers. Taking sensible precautions like those recommended by the Foreign and Commonwealth Office (www.fco.gov.uk) will help you avoid many problems by taking good care of yourself and your belongings. First off, there are good habits to adopt, particularly at vulnerable times such as when you first arrive in a country or are sightseeing in lively crowds.

LAURA'S TIPS: Keeping safe

✓ Carry only the minimum amount of cash that you need each day.

✓ Avoid opening your purse or wallet in a crowd. If you must, keep your back to a wall or ask a companion to shield you from onlookers.

✓ Adopt a strict habit of leaving your valuables and spare cash in the hotel safe.

✓ If there is no hotel safe, keep your passport pouch close to your skin at all times.

✓ Do not flaunt your wealth by wearing flashy jewellery or an expensive watch

✓ Avoid unlit streets and alleyways at night.

✓ Never resist violent theft — just hand over your valuables.

✓ Never pack valuables into your checked-in luggage.

✓ Keep a secret stash of $100 taped inside your case for emergencies.

Fran had barely started her trip when a thief struck. At only her second stop in Sydney she got a very unpleasant surprise:

'One morning I went for my breakfast and when I got back to my room my leather wallet had disappeared. I don't know if I'd locked my room. It was one of those push-button things and I just don't know. I lost all my personal notes, my flight itinerary, my passport, the lot. Luckily my son had scanned everything and put it on my travelling email. I was leaving very early Tuesday morning so I went to stay with an old friend on the Sunshine Coast for the weekend. When I met my old friend Sally I just burst into tears – she thought I was crying to see her after so many years! In the end I got a temporary 12-month passport. But I lost all my currency, about £170. And all the paperwork and all the notes I made on places to see and the walks I wanted to do.'

Joanne, on the other hand, had been travelling for a few months when her concentration slipped in Arrivals at Denpasar Bali Airport:

'I still don't know if my bank card was stolen or if I lost it. No one ever took any money out of my account. I arrived at the airport in Bali with my son George and got some new currency out of a machine, then got in a taxi and next day I couldn't find the card. The real pain was that I hadn't brought the emergency number with me to cancel it. I had to email my boyfriend in the UK and he sorted it out. My next problem was that George only had a few traveller's cheques left so our budget dropped to about £20 a day. It was fun in some ways as we stayed at homestays but in retrospect it was stupid. I had plenty of money in my savings account but with just one bank card and no backup we were forced into silly debates like whether we could afford another mango juice or not.'

Violent attack is something all travellers rightly fear. As an intrepid traveller, Polly knew that 'a long trip always has highs and lows'. One of her lows came while volunteering in South Africa:

'I was mugged when a couple of companions and I were returning to our car after a night out. As I reached the car door I was grabbed from behind and my bag was ripped from across my shoulder. The guy had been hiding in the shadows and moved in before any of us knew what was happening. He'd probably been standing there a long time and when he saw me it was a gift, a "mama" with a disability and a bag was too good to miss. As I'd been out earlier that day my bag contained my digital camera and my prescription sunglasses. The amount of money in the bag was not a lot by our standards but more than a week's wages to someone from a township. The event was upsetting but none of us was hurt except for bruising to my shoulder. We were lucky as often this type of crime is accompanied by an indiscriminate knife or gun attack.'

THE FACTS: Theft and losses

- If your money, passport or anything else is stolen, report it at once to the local police or to the airport authorities if the theft occurs in transit.

- Obtain an official statement about the loss: you will need one to claim against your insurance.

- Money – phone your bank at home to transfer money or cancel your credit card using the relevant 24-hour emergency number.

- Traveller's cheques – contact the issuing agent.

- Tickets – see your local tour representative or airline agent.

- Passport – apply to the local British Consul for a temporary replacement.

- Mobile phone – ring your provider and put a stop on the phone.

Polly admits that she had grown less vigilant after being in Africa for some time. Complacency is clearly a danger once the novelty of travelling has worn off.

Day 50 Galle, Sri Lanka

The Foreign and Commonwealth website lists Sri Lanka's threat level as orange – it advises against *all* travel to certain parts of the country. I've rather optimistically assumed that all trouble will be confined to the battle zone in the north east. Orange alert is the same level as Indonesia where I've seen no trouble at all – but it's also the same as the current warning for Iraq, Afghanistan and Iran.

Sadly, now I've arrived I can see Sri Lanka looks like a country torn apart by civil war. There are soldiers carrying guns at the airport, machine gun embrasures up on the sandbagged walls, and big guns that look as shiny as plastic toys ('No sudden movements, they're real,' I tell myself nervously) in the hands of the military police who slow down my taxi. 'Welcome to Paradise Island,' says my taxi driver as a stony-faced policeman waves us on. Can he be serious?

Then there's the rain, a torrent of water that chills and covers the old port of Galle with blackened slime. After learning that my grandparents travelled here in the 1920s I had imagined Galle to be some dreamy colonial fort-town. I was expecting white villas and verandas with trays of Planter's Punch instead of the old arches mouldy with damp that seem to surround the town. I think the kindest description of how I feel is Culture Fatigue. Like many victims of theft I feel bitterly uncommunicative for a few paranoid days. Everywhere I go strange men stop in their tracks, stare and begin to walk beside me making annoyingly intrusive conversation. I have perfected an eyes-fixed-straight-ahead glare as I hurry onwards, refusing to speak. There are few other tourists in this tsunami and terrorist-battered country. Hardly the perfect setting for a romantic reunion, I mutter to myself as I stomp miserably along the slippery streets.

My disorientation is complete when I am generously invited to meet the family at my hospitable but gloomy homestay. The extended family are gathering for a wedding feast that I unfortunately can't attend due to the urgent need to get back to Colombo airport to report my camera theft. Going down to dinner I find huddles of robed young women carrying babies milling around the sitting room. A child is led up to me at bedtime and looks so terrified that I decline kissing her goodnight like the rest of the family and gently pat the poor thing on her head. My dinner at this cookery-famed homestay is lovely: chicken curry, split pea dhal, fresh pineapple and doughy fresh flat breads. But as I eat, the busy family brush past me, a cat winds around my leg and an old man staggers past and belches. Then I'm introduced to a patriarchal old man who, despite our polite chit-chat about his recent trip to London and Oxford, can't help but remind me of a very famous person. With his long white beard, cap and robes I'm making small talk with a striking lookalike of Osama Bin Ladin himself.

I don't generally seek out other Brits but in a moment of good fortune I bump into Mary-Ann and Michael at what seems to be the only café open in town. They are here for three months, checking out property with a view to early retirement in the sun. But even in their first week they have seen and heard about disturbing incidents. A few days earlier they saw shrapnel in the wall at the scene of a recent suicide bomb attack in Colombo and report that areas of the city are cordoned off by the police. We discuss the absence of tourists, the rain and the irritating plague of touts. 'Everyone's trying to sell you something because there are so few tourists and they can see you're travelling independently. Now I just tell them 'I'm with the tour group," quips Michael. We agree to get in touch later and I wonder how they will get on for three months as virtually the only tourists in the area. When I tell them I'll be in New Zealand for the New Year, Mary-Ann looks wistful. I can't help but sense she's less comfortable with the uneasy atmosphere than Michael.

Safety first

The international news, with its catalogue of warfare, bombings and natural disasters could deter even the most adventurous traveller. But the fact is that you are far more likely to lose your passport or be a victim of a traffic accident than be caught up in a terrorist attack. Unlike foreign visitors to Britain who cancel travel to all of Britain after an incident in one isolated area, the trick is to try to locate the real danger zones beneath the eye-catching headline. Then if it's a serious incident, be flexible. Change your plans and be glad that at least you have these choices in life. Checking ahead will do much to lessen the risks of getting caught up in violence or being stranded in a country where normal services have ceased.

Charles and Elize's luxury itinerary included time in Nepal but as they watched their hotel television CNN news announced that a coup was taking place:

> 'Our agent in London contacted us and said the FCO site had announced that travel to Nepal was not recommended. A guide told us we would like a beautiful spa in the foothills of the Himalayas so we went there and then on to Corbett National Park. We were sorry we didn't go to Nepal as we had wanted to go to Kathmandu and to see the national parks. The good thing was that the tour operator not only made the decision for us but also made all the alternative arrangements for us. Their agent in India immediately came to see us and gave us new vouchers so we didn't have to do a thing.'

Without a tour operator or even a television to watch in their budget homestays, Joanne and George had no idea that anti-western riots had broken out at their next destination – the Islamic island of Lombok:

> 'We had actually bought our bus tickets to the ferry port to Lombok when we started to hear rumours from other travellers. My son George was still up for it and wanted to charter a boat once the ferry was cancelled – that's the recklessness of youth for you! Then we spoke to a group of newly returned Dutch travellers who warned us not to go under any circumstances. They told us tourists were being shot and western hotels had been set on fire. With no set itinerary we just got out the guide book and chose another island to head for – Nusa Lembongan to the south of Bali.'

Few people would consider travelling directly to the area of a natural disaster only a couple of days after it occurred. But after some careful checking Josh took a gamble to ignore the global media story and trust local knowledge instead. Josh had booked a plane ticket into Bali just after Christmas 2004. On Boxing Day morning he watched the television news of the Asian tsunami with an increasing sense of horror:

> 'By lunchtime my airline contacted me and said they would refund my flight. However, there was a problem. I was going to meet a girlfriend in Bali and she had unrefundable flights from Singapore and was due to set off in 72 hours. I had also paid a chunk of my savings directly to the hotel in Bali over the internet and I was pretty sure I wouldn't get it back. I wondered if it would be completely crazy to ignore the warnings and still fly into Indonesia?

> 'Scouring the internet for information over the next 24 hours revealed a different picture. The news was showing a map of

Indonesia with earthquake tremors radiating out from its centre but in fact the epicentre was Aceh, far to the west. I managed to contact someone living in Bali via a newsgroup and learned there was no impact whatsoever in Bali. I did a double check with a friend at an airline who confirmed that Bali was completely untouched. My first emotional response had been to cancel the trip – it felt frightening, reckless and incredibly selfish to go holidaying on the fringes of a huge natural disaster. Yet my rational brain said, why not go?

'One pressing reason to cancel remained. By flying into a country subject to a Foreign Office warning I was told I would invalidate my travel insurance. But frantic texts revealed my girlfriend still

LAURA'S TIPS: Avoiding danger spots

✓ Be security conscious and take sensible precautions. Be prepared to change direction if you hear of danger ahead.

✓ Be alert to unattended baggage in public places.

✓ Look out for people acting suspiciously near 'western' institutions.

✓ Avoid all political and other demonstrations or gatherings.

✓ Keep updated about the local and regional political scene in the media or on internet news sites.

wanted to go. Rather scared by now, I decided to stick to my plan and fly off without insurance into Indonesia on 30 December, four days after the tsunami.

'In fact we found Bali utterly untouched by the dramatic earthquake and at least found we could pay for emergency supplies that were shipped off to Aceh and delivered by truck within 48 hours. Yet would I do it again? Probably not. Still, I learned that the big media story often conflates the scenes of disasters with other better-known names on a map.'

Day 52 Colombo, Sri Lanka

How do you get things done in this country? The night before my husband Laurence arrives I achieve a small miracle and book into the luxurious Taj Airport Hotel to enjoy some private pampering. The Taj is a real treat: homestays have been fascinating but I've got a hankering for indulgence. At last I get a bubble bath, hairdryer, movie channel and fridge-cold Mars Bar. Bliss.

Officially the hotel is full. After learning this I glumly asked around at the airport where a rep mysteriously scribbled a chit to book me a room. I've since been offered the same room half-price by a taxi driver. Sri Lanka as a travel destination baffles me – the country needs tourists so badly but getting things booked always involves touts and kickbacks, a system that leaves me exasperated. My tour operator is also the first of his ilk who can't deliver what he promised. He insists he can't get our rail tickets up to the hill country or book certain hotels despite most of them looking eerily empty. I'm furious.

Next morning I'm awake at 5am to welcome Laurence at the chaotic airport. It's been seven weeks since we last saw each other and at first we both seem shy and awkward. Laurence is in a strange state: shell-shocked by his father's death and a teaching term so frustrating he has resigned from most of his job to start a difficult transition to freelance work. All this has left him tired and run down while I feel guilty that I've dragged him to this troubled and chaotic country.

Day 54 Kandy, Sri Lanka

A few days later, after staying at the 5-star Earl's Regency Hotel in Kandy, we've shared the ups and downs of the recent months and are both more comfortable to be back together as a couple. As I get news of friends and family back home I feel pangs of homesickness for the first time. I think of crisp winter mornings, our comfortable home and my mum and family. Then I see fogbound Heathrow on the television news and Laurence tells me about the shopping frenzy and dreary dark mornings. As the long rains cease we sit out around the pool in the sun and I think – yes, there's nothing that can't wait back at home in England.

Day 56 Nuwara Eliya, Sri Lanka

At home I'm a tea addict, drinking mug after mug of the strong, dark stuff as I work. So a trip to Sri Lanka's Tea Country has an added appeal, to see how my favourite tipple is grown. The road up to Nuwara Eliya has to be one of the worst of my travels – our pre-booked railway tickets never do turn up so instead we have to be driven up half-finished roads littered with boulders from earth-slips. Climbing ever higher in our worryingly overheating car, we reach the lush highlands created as 'little England'. Women tea-pickers in colourful saris bend forward, rapidly plucking the acres of green leaves and casting them backwards into the sacks on their backs. At a tea factory the leaves undergo a relatively simple process of drying, fermenting and sorting. Many workers are originally Tamils from South India, dark-faced and lean, with gold nose-studs in their strong faces.

Later, we relax at Nuwara Eliya's elegant Grand Hotel. At 6,000ft the hill country is seasonally cold in December. It takes me a shivering half-hour to work out that the ironwork fireplace in our room actually glows and throws out heat by the flick of a switch. Before dinner we huddle up to the open fire in the lounge and I miss my warm winter clothes. The Planter's Punch is pleasant but I'm looking forward to hot soup and rice and curry. And after all that, a warming cup of tea is the perfect nightcap.

Day 58 Christmas Day Nuwara Eliya, Sri Lanka

White Christmas, Jingle Bells and even best forgotten ditties like *The Christmas Polka* tinkle non-stop from our hotel's speakers. There are cotton wool snowmen, polystyrene Santa's sleighs and even a plywood elves' grotto in our hotel lobby. Christmas is a festival we expected to escape from. In fact, Laurence and I agreed not even to buy gifts as we've both been busy and our reunion is the best present ever. And OK, I admit it – I'm already carrying well over my 20kg luggage limit.

Our shared Christmas present arrives in a chance to explore the amazing World Heritage sites in the island's Cultural Triangle. Even better, with Laurence taking over as photographer I can get over my sadness at losing my camera. As he enthuses over shots of ancient cities I reflect that thankfully my sisters took photos through most of our tour of Indonesia. I've lost some wonderful images of Africa and India but I'm fit, healthy and ready to plough on with the trip.

First off is Dambulla, a Buddhist cave complex atop a mountain that moves us with its solemn atmosphere of centuries of worship. Next we visit Sigiriya, the massive lion rock that dominates the plain like a crouching giant. Here the public holiday means the site is crowded – in fact the antiquated iron stairways feel dangerously overcrowded. I chicken out of climbing to the top but Laurence decides to clamber up with the milling crowds. He reports back that it was an ordeal: the stairway narrowed to inches wide, and the descending crowd overspilled into those climbing up. Then one of the local pests struck, a 'helping hand' from a tout prompted an angry demand for the usual fee of 1000 rupiah (about £5). Stranded hundreds of feet above the ground on a few inches of iron is not the best location to be harangued by the locals so Laurence did his best to haggle down the amount. Then he was accused of not handing over the agreed amount of 300 rupiahs. Minutes later the snake charmer who Laurence has snapped runs after us, unhappy with his tip and shouting for his fiver, too. Even though we try to tip fairly we're getting tired of people bullying us into giving them money.

After a tour of the ruined city of Polonnaruwa we visit our final site, the lost city of Anuradhapura where giant stoupas stand as impressive as any pyramid of Egypt. Here our view of the Sri Lankans is softened by meeting some gentle young monks. They want to be photographed worshipping at the Reclining Buddha and we agree to email the beautiful images to their monastery. Not a cent is asked for and we fleetingly feel like real people and not just western wallets on legs. It's a pity our driver couldn't follow her example. He drops Laurence off at the airport first and then returns to pick me up for my later flight. We're both flying on to Auckland but over the busy Christmas season getting on the same flight was impossible. After taking my generous tip the driver insists Laurence has forgotten to pay back a loan for one of our many entrance fees. Too polite for my own good I hand over another stash of notes. Of course I later discover that Laurence doesn't owe him any more money. Honestly – we've been scammed to the last, even by our own over-tipped driver.

THE FACTS: Top scams

The vast majority of people in the world genuinely wish their tourist visitors well. However, in some countries you may encounter a troubling number of attempts to free you from your cash. The methods change all the time but are often variations on these age old tricks:

- Distraction – a stranger spills liquid on you or thrusts a baby in your face. While distracted an accomplice picks your pocket.

- Credit card fraud – a shopkeeper takes your card to a back room and swipes it twice. Always insist on watching the transaction.

- Money exchange – there are as many con methods as there are playing card tricks but they all result in you being short-changed. If you can't find an official bank, take a friend to witness the exchange and count your money before you leave.

- Gem or antique purchase – if you are ever offered any 'too good to be true' deal – it is.

- The worthy student – highly plausible 'students' may approach you with a sorry tale about expensive fees. Sadly, your money is far more likely to support organised crime.

- Taxi fares – don't get in a taxi unless you can agree a price in advance. If there are language problems write the figure down.

- The bogus policeman – after being inveigled into accepting a counterfeit coin, cigarettes, drugs or alcohol, a policeman swoops down upon you. Unsurprisingly, he is likely to accept a large bribe to drop charges.

- The fake travel agent – you buy a tour or other service that doesn't materialise. Always try to book in person at a recommended office.

Avoiding accidents and illness

Falling ill on holiday was something I'd dreaded. Before setting off I'd pictured myself collapsing over a filthy foreign toilet, not knowing which end of my body to direct at the toilet bowl. In the event, I've avoided most of the usual lurgies. After almost 60 days travelling I've had two minor falls, one as a result of that holiday classic – slipping on a wet tiled bathroom floor – and the other stumbling over a kerb. On Java, climbing terrifying Mount Bromo at dawn after a night's indulgence in western food and wine brought on some Olympic-class running into the bushes with short-lived diarrhoea. Throwing rubbish into a bin in Java I was horrified to slash my finger on some torn metal but rapid cleaning with antiseptic handspray and a plaster prevented any septic complications. Apart from that I've only had the dratted cold in Bali that clearly shrank my brain cells and led me to pack my camera in my case.

Most travellers avoid serious illness or accidents. Taking the medical precautions and simple kit outlined in Chapter Four will launch you well on the road to a healthy trip. Once your trip has started, it's nevertheless important to exercise some basic precautions that should keep you fit enough to enjoy every day of your adventure.

Ajay, a 63-year-old doctor, offers a simple and sensible prescription to staying healthy:

> 'I took mefloqine, an anti-malarial. I ate in clean hotels and restaurants. I stuck to mineral water even for brushing my teeth. I had no health problems.'

Nevertheless, the occasional stomach bug is always a possibility. Preventative measures include using anti-bacterial handwashes, using a toothbrush cover, avoiding ice in drinks and only eating hot, freshly cooked food. Carrying an anti-diarrhoea tablet in your moneybelt will also be a godsend if you get caught midway on a long journey. Bananas, yogurt, flat Coca-Cola and plain rice are all popular remedies to get you back on your feet as quickly as possible.

Proving that the amount you spend will not necessarily protect you from illness, Charles fell ill with a gastric bug on the P&O cruise out to Mumbai. Elize managed to control her symptoms with a quick dose of Imodium but the sickness rapidly spread through the ship:

> 'Charles was confined to ship for 48 hours and unfortunately missed the trip to Cairo. He got the bug and was being sick all over the place. One night we were in our cabin and a team of masked nurses came in to give him injections and I was just lying next to him – it was quite surreal. Even the Daily Mail picked up the story as some people had it quite badly, especially elderly people.'

On trips of a year or longer, some physical wear and tear is inevitable. As Kate and Keith found out, hiring a motorbike is always a risk:

> 'I happened to lean against Keith's motorbike – he heard my flesh sizzle before my pain receptors kicked in. I had leaned up against his exhaust with my bare leg and burnt it to buggery.'

Sue was also living life to the full when a minor accident struck:

> 'I hurt my ribs on a power boat trip while pulling up the ladder. This was the day before a four-by-four 18–35s adventure trip. (No, I didn't lie about my age!) I should have taken off my bum bag as the buckle got caught under my ribs. It was very painful.'

Jean also had to sample New Zealand health services when her heart condition flared up:

LAURA'S TIPS: Staying healthy

✓ Avoid too much sun. Adopt the Australian slogan — Slip, Slap, Slop. Slip on a T-shirt, Slap on a hat and Slop on some sunscreen.

✓ Keep hydrated. Make clean drinking water a priority and where tap water is unsafe, use your own supply to clean your teeth.

✓ Eat in places that look clean and choose food that is freshly cooked.

✓ Wear insect repellent spray and long sleeves and trousers in the evening.

✓ Avoid over-exertion. Expect tropical heat to sap your energy until you are acclimatised. Build rest days into your itinerary.

✓ Practise safe sex. Always use a condom with new partners.

✓ Avoid excessive alcohol.

✓ Do not be tempted to use drugs. Not only will you be vulnerable to theft or worse, but in many gap year countries the penalty can be death.

'I had to have treatment at Timaru Hospital and was dealt with speedily. There was no payment as there is a reciprocal agreement with the UK.'

Sometimes medical services are just not available and falling ill means making quick decisions about a change of direction. Polly was ill while spending a few weeks travelling alone by bus through Zululand to Swaziland. After getting soaked in the rain she found herself alone in a very basic hostel:

'I had developed some kind of chest infection and was feeling pretty rough. I thought a few days' rest would soon put me right but with the wet conditions there was no improvement and I knew I had to get some antibiotics. Also, the mosquitoes had feasted well on me and malaria is a big problem in Swaziland. As my resources were lowered with the infection I was at greater risk of getting malaria. It was time to move on and my journey to Mozambique would have to wait for another time.'

Also living under very basic conditions in Africa, Emrys suffered the consequences of his 'total immersion' lifestyle. During his two-year trip he succeeded in sampling a whole series of grisly diseases: typhoid, amoebic dysentery and, ultimately, malaria:

'You can use repellent and you can sleep under a net but if 95% of the population has malaria there's a good chance the mosqui-toes are carrying it. I was taking tablets at that time and was lying in a hotel when I developed fairly classic symptoms. I started gig-gling because I felt like one of those people in a classic film run-ning with sweat and shivering. Next day I went to the doctor and got some treatment on an outpatient basis. That was the only time I had the full-blown symptoms. I've still got malarial anti-bodies which is one reason they won't let me give blood.'

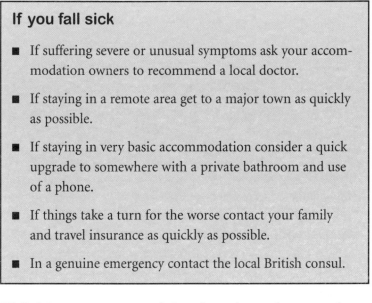

If you fall sick

- If suffering severe or unusual symptoms ask your accommodation owners to recommend a local doctor.

- If staying in a remote area get to a major town as quickly as possible.

- If staying in very basic accommodation consider a quick upgrade to somewhere with a private bathroom and use of a phone.

- If things take a turn for the worse contact your family and travel insurance as quickly as possible.

- In a genuine emergency contact the local British consul.

While it is common sense to bring along plenty of your usual prescription medicines and optical prescription, you might not give your foot health such a high priority. When George went backpacking with his mother Joanne, he had to learn the hard way how crucial his special podiatric insoles were to his wellbeing:

'A real lowpoint was losing my foot insoles in a hostel in Sydney three months into the trip. This caused me to suffer great pain in my feet and seriously affected my travelling enjoyment after a week. It was so bad I had serious thoughts about returning home as I wouldn't be able to work in that condition. I tried a few ineffective cures on Bali including massage and even a scary visit to a village shaman. Luckily, on my return to Sydney I found an expensive private podiatrist who made some new insoles which got rid of the pain and enabled me to resume work and enjoy my adventures.'

George hadn't taken out any medical insurance for his trip, naively trusting that at 29 years old he'd be fit and healthy. Fortunately, the cost of his private treatment was only a few hundred dollars. But when things go wrong in a big way, health insurance will always prove to be one of your most important purchases. Elize found this out the year before her big trip to India when she took on a contract in Russia:

'One snowy day in March I was looking around art galleries with a friend during my time off. I slipped over a manhole cover that was thick with sheet ice and fell backwards onto the edge of the metal cover. After an x-ray I was told to just rest and that it was fine. I carried on working for another month but despite physio my back was getting more and more painful. Eventually, I landed out in a Russian hospital after an MRI scan showed a fractured vertebra. The hospital said I needed to travel as a stretcher case back to the UK but fortunately, as I was working on a contract assisting Aeroflot, a few favours were asked and I managed to get two seats in Club Class. The hospital arranged for an ambulance to take me to the airport and I was carried on a stretcher through the airport.

'At Heathrow I was wheeled out in a wheelchair and Charles was there to meet me and take me to the hospital. Thankfully, the doctor told me that if I wore a spinal corset for a few weeks I could recuperate at home. The costs were incredible: the clinic was talking about tens of thousands of pounds for the flight arrangements. I had to put all my medical costs on my American Express card, keep all the receipts and have it all reimbursed later. It just doesn't bear thinking about having an accident like that without insurance. It could happen to anybody, with costs suddenly spiralling out of control.'

Getting help abroad

British consular services (and the British High Commission in Commonwealth countries) will not appreciate being pestered about trivial matters but they will help Brits in real difficulty. If you need help in a country where there is no British presence you should get help from the offices of another European Union state or from Australian or New Zealand representatives.

THE FACTS: Consular services

WHAT THEY CAN DO

- Issue replacement passports.

- Provide information about transferring funds if you lose your money.

- Provide help if you have suffered rape or serious assault, are a victim of crime, or are in hospital.

- Provide details of local lawyers, interpreters, doctors and funeral directors.

- Do their best to contact you within 24 hours of being told that you have been detained.

- Contact your family or friends for you.

WHAT THEY CANNOT DO

- In general they cannot get involved in criminal proceedings, for example to get you out of prison.

- They cannot get involved in immigration issues.

- Give you money or pay your bills (or if they, do it will be a loan).

HOMEWARD BOUND

Day 60 Auckland, New Zealand

This is my 17th flight and any pleasure I had ever felt from spending the night on a plane disappeared months ago. This time, the 13-hour overnighter from Singapore to Auckland has seats that are cramped and babies that are very loud. Then the woman next to me starts to vomit in a bag. And the babies scream louder. Why on earth would anyone think flying is glamorous? Pass me the sick bag . . .

Of course, the point of flying really is the destination and I need to remember it once took around five months of hell and heaving water to get here from the UK. Waiting to meet Chris at Auckland International on Boxing Day, I'm at one of the great iconic meeting points in the world. A big screen over the Arrivals gate shows close-up images of newly arrived visitors while crowds with 'Welcome Home' balloons, banners and flowers scan each newcomer's face expectantly. People of seemingly every nation are reuniting: Indians, Malaysians, Chinese, Italians, Brits, Arabs. Yet the gestures are all the same – the cries of delight, the open arms, the heartfelt hugs. There are new grandchildren to admire and old-timers to welcome with a gentle pat of the head.

Chris arrives and we enjoy our own hugs and grins of recognition. After nearly nine weeks in the tropics it's suddenly a relief to arrive in New Zealand's cool fresh air, free of terror alerts, squat toilets and soupy humidity. Then Laurence comes through Arrivals and along with the rest of the crowd we celebrate humanity's best side, and spring together with laughter, big grins and loving hugs.

Day 61 Waiheke Island, New Zealand

Hanging out a clean load of washing on the line had never before struck me as bliss, but it's the little domestic things I've come to miss. After months of hotels and homestays there is something so liberating about renting a house – no breakfast times to get up for, no polite chit-chat, no worries about unexpected bills. I can't believe my luck in renting such a beautiful place as Garden Hideaway on Waiheke Island simply from clicking an image on the internet. It's a kauri wood house with huge gardens down to the ocean, three pretty bedrooms and views across the gulf that change every moment from sunrise to sunset.

Meals are relaxed affairs out on the deck in the sun and even washing up is enjoyable. Now that's a sentence I never thought I would write! Everything exceeds our expectations: there are steps down to a rocky beach, a hammock and lots of faded garden furniture. It's also a place where we can invite people over, share lunch and imagine for a few special days that we actually live this laid-back Waiheke Island lifestyle.

Day 64 New Year's Eve Waiheke Island, New Zealand

'Like Enid Blyton's *Famous Five* island with vineyards,' says Laurence, as we explore Waiheke's endless vistas of tiny coves and rocky headlands. The local kids, however, are rather more sun-bleached than George, Timmy and co, and zip around in their own motorised dinghies. The cafés are funky with rows of wine glasses clinking from breakfast-time onwards and the dress code is flip-flops, faded shorts and unruly hair.

Our New Year's Eve is simple: Waiheke has no fireworks or fiestas. We kick off with a hilarious boules match on the lawn between me and Laurence and Chris and his girlfriend Lucy. Then we opt for an Indian feast at the local independent cinema. After that Laurence and I struggle to keep our eyes open as all this fresh oxygen has us keeling over by 11pm. Chris and Lucy go out to see Auckland's soaring glass harbour front and futuristic Sky Tower across the gulf, shimmering like Sky City in *Star Wars*. Above it, fireworks blossom silently and distantly across the water. Another year is ended and I have only three weeks of travelling left. It's magical to share this peace and beauty, thousands of miles from the usual drunken crowds and mumbled renditions of *Auld Lang Syne*.

Day 71 Milford, New Zealand

In New Zealand's South Island we've done some of the best walks of our lives. Last week we retraced the scene of one of the classic elvish chase scenes from *The Lord of the Rings* while staying near the aptly named Paradise. Following a clear and easy track across swing bridges into magical forests we explored an unspoilt wilderness beside roaring, milky turquoise torrents.

Now, after a peaceful week on the shores of gorgeous Lake Te Anau, we've just walked the final stretch of the Routeburn Track. The sky above is china blue and the ferns around us chlorophyll green – New Zealand has shockingly bright natural colours unfiltered by pollution and magnified by the radiant sunshine. From a cool shady start Laurence and I have climbed hand in hand, zigzagging up the mountain until our legs ache. It feels good for my lungs to be pumping sweet New Zealand air as we approach Key Summit. Miraculously, snowy peaks appear barely an arm's length away, glittering in the afternoon sunshine. At the summit I throw myself down and crash out with my back supported by tonnes of granite mountain, feeling my heart pound with exhilaration. I feel simply on top of the world.

Feeling great

A number of factors account for grown-up gappers returning home feeling better than they have felt for years. For starters, most travellers will have spent far more time out of doors than at home and most feel fitter and stronger. Avoiding the dark winters in the UK must be one of the best tonics against every ailment from depression to arthritis. There's the mental stimulation too, from the ever-changing backdrop of different countries and cultures. There's also a boost to self-esteem in carrying out long-nurtured goals. I also suspect there is an element of reinvention when we travel. At home, we might have reputations as routine-bound fuddy-duddies but travel allows us to be someone rather more interesting, someone alert and open to change. We leave our boring personas behind and are more prepared to have a go – whether it's meeting interesting locals or fellow travellers or doing that bungee jump or mountain hike. And if there's one secret of youth it's that – staying fresh, open to new ideas and flexible in mind and body.

Feeling younger was what 54-year-old Tim enthused about. Taking off to Morocco powerfully reinvigorated both his mind and body:

> 'The benefits have been new attitudes, new direction, new me. My health greatly improved throughout the trip. Fresh air, fresh food, little or no pollution, no chemicals or E additives in food, no alcohol. I also gave up smoking and took exercise (not a lot though!).'

Kate and Keith also found time away from Britain allowed them to profoundly rethink their lives and attitudes:

'It has literally given us the opportunity of breaking our circle of being and doing things a bit differently on our own terms when planning for the next stage of our lives. We also met some wonderful people and have reached a new level of tolerance and understanding of others. We are lighter (physically and mentally), very chilled out and very happy.'

Fran is rightly proud of her achievement in travelling so far on her own when most of her contemporaries are content with television soaps and slippers. To her advantage she started the trip with a good level of fitness, spending her time as a volunteer leading up to six 1.5-hour walks a week:

'The trip means so much to me. I'm just a little bit sad that I didn't do it when I was younger. But I am so pleased that I just decided to do it and go. In one shop in Ubud the girls asked me how old I was. When I told her 70, she said, "No, not that age. Balinese lady of 70 all bent over." Not me.'

Joanne too, returned feeling better than she had done for years:

'Time away doing my own thing felt extraordinary. Being with my son George was also incredibly rejuvenating. One of my highlights was clubbing all night on Bondi Beach on New Year's Eve and getting home at 6am. I wouldn't have believed I was capable! It was subtle things too – allowing myself to laze around all day chatting to other travellers and spontaneously going off wherever we fancied. That's how young people behave and that's how I learned to be. It was like a last Indian summer of my late youth/early middle age.'

Day 80 Lahaina, Maui, Hawaii, USA

Despite feeling physically well and fit, I have developed one serious complaint – homesickness. With just one week left, time with Laurence and Chris has jolted me out of my independent mood. Laurence will fly straight home one day after me and get back to Britain while I'm still in Hawaii. The heartbreaking bit was leaving my son Chris behind in Auckland with no idea when we'll next meet. We both found ourselves lingering for a final glimpse of each other in the airport lobby. In the end we made three attempts to part, Chris lingering by the exit and me hovering by a pillar. It was horrible: my heart strings felt stretched taut as wire.

Crossing the international dateline somewhere between Fiji and Honolulu has left me absolutely baffled about the time. To make matters worse there's the hardline attitude of US immigration's homeland security to contend with. In Honolulu all of us sleepy passengers (including the majority destined for Vancouver) are woken up, marched off the plane and corralled into a holding room to be photographed and have our fingerprints scanned.

Hawaii does look beautiful from the air as I take a tiny local airplane over to the smaller island of Maui where I'm staying. There's a perfect volcanic crater of wrinkled brown far below me amidst an ocean of every shade of blue from aquamarine to peacock. But down on the ground my first impressions are disappointing: men in Hawaiian shirts and sun-damaged women in miniskirts with bleached hair and gigantic jewellery. I just can't get in the groove here in Hawaii. Firstly, it's that environment all solo travellers dread, a prime honeymoon destination. I'd love a romantic break here but really don't want to stare out at the sunset on my own. Not only that, but the local Polynesian culture is reduced to tacky hula shows performed for crowds of vacationing Americans taking time off their cruise ships.

I remember the Ngoa tribe who danced for us in Flores before their village meeting. Money, real estate and over-sized sports vehicles seem to be the gods here.

Day 82 Lahaina, Maui, Hawaii, USA

It's my last day on Maui before flying home and I've been taking it easy, enjoying the lovely 40-minute walk into town to see a few last sights and visit the hairdresser. I put it down to homesickness but I've turned into a bit of a Grumpy Old Woman. I've been trying to live out my dream as an assured travel writer, booking a top lunch by the beach with my notepad at the ready on a crisp linen table-cloth. But the food is fatty and overcooked after the fresh fiery flavours of New Zealand and Asia. I find myself shaking my head at the bikini-clad and baggy-shorted teenagers on the beach learn-ing to surf, playing Frisbee and strumming guitars. It's another brand of paradise here, compared to everything I've seen: a strangely self-regarding lifestyle, like lotus-eaters blind to all but their own patch of sand.

All travelled out

It seems to happen to many long-term travellers after a while. However idyllic the open road appears at first, the urge simply to go home finally takes over. After a year away, Kate and Keith ditched their plan to spend a further year exploring South America:

> 'We have decided to use our return ticket and go back to England and see how we feel for the next year. We are both travelled out – and ready for some reality and some grimness. You don't appreci-ate things when they are wonderful all the time. No more packing and unpacking, it's time to light the home fires.'

Joanne also cut short her trip, although only by a few weeks:

'Back in Oz in the New Year I suddenly felt it was time to go home. I was holding back George who had a working visa, and Australia is a pretty expensive place to coast along with no income. I was also desperate to see my new boyfriend after three months and find out if the relationship was real or just some email romance.'

For Michael and Mary-Ann, who intended to spend three months in Sri Lanka, it was a continuing unease with the state of the country that led them to abandon their original plan:

'Sri Lanka was very disappointing. We did intend to spend three months beach-hopping down the west coast but we couldn't find any idyllic beaches. Also the locals don't leave you alone, they are always trying to hatch a plan to make some money out of you. So we decided to cut our losses and fly to Goa to see a decent beach and for a bit of a buzz.'

Maybe my mood reflects being off colour again, with a bad cold and a throat that feels like it has razor blades in it. As I swelter up the last few blocks home to my studio apartment, my mind is fixated on a welcome lie-down with the aircon blasting over me. But it is not to be. When I open my room it's crammed with someone else's suitcases and possessions. Apparently, on this very last night of my whole trip, I've made a mistake with my booking and am now homeless. Kim, the owner, has scooped up my things and put them outside in the baking hot yard. I am not a happy guest, despite the owner's slogan 'No Disappointments'. I'm plenty disappointed with the owners but also maddened by my own mistake.

Feeling like some red-faced destitute bag lady, I move into a cramped bedroom in a local hippy woman's house with added extras of highway noise and car alarms to keep me awake half the night. That international dateline has a lot to answer for, I groan, as I repack yet again, feeling stress palpitations mingle with my feverish cold. Can I just be teleported home now, please?

Day 83 Honolulu, Hawaii, USA

Honolulu is famous for its traffic jams so, after reluctantly hiring a car on my last day, I decide not to travel too far, just to Pearl Harbour. The experience isn't as sentimental as I expected, just a blandly non-judgmental film about the Japanese bombings (the Japanese are one of the largest groups of visitors) and a short boat ride to the monument where I see the battleship USS Arizona rusting beneath me, the tomb of more than a thousand dead. It is in fact very moving.

Then of course I join the highway in the wrong direction and find myself motoring far away from Honolulu's skyscrapers and airport. Whoa, I mustn't miss that plane. Terrified behind the wheel of my over-sized car, it seems to take forever to backtrack while deciphering the map in the middle of four-lane rush hour traffic. But – hallelujah! – I find the obscure backstreet lot and get a shuttle to the airport. Breathlessly I watch the sun set over Honolulu and think of the thousands of miles still ahead of me. I hear it's snowing in New York so I've got my fleece and some new tracksuit bottoms at the ready and I've just checked my bag through to Manchester – hooray! I can't stop grinning to think I'll soon see Laurence, my family, my friends and my home.

Day 84 New York, USA

I can't hold back the tears as I listen to a sentimental song on my earphones as my flight arcs high above New York. I've just spent five long hours at New York's Liberty Airport watching the snow fall beyond gigantic windows, surrounded by swarms of dark-suited commuters. Now I feel full to the brim of tender longing for Laurence but also moved to see the spectacle of Manhattan twinkling like a city of stars at the edge of the continent. The Statue of Liberty shines far below me, a symbol of all that has been great about America and its historic welcome to people of every creed and colour. Now I'm cruising above New Jersey, an amber crisscross of roadways and bridges glimpsed through gossamer trails of cloud. Looking back on the trip I'm so glad I've done it. I want to be a person who takes opportunities and not someone who says 'I wish I had'. I don't regret a second.

As New Jersey makes way for the black void of the Atlantic I get a sudden sense of the whole globe spinning beneath me. Falling into a reverie I see a silent tumble of images: of tiny white-toothed children grinning around us in Indonesia, of scaly dragons flicking man-killing tails, a blue Delft tile caught in an old lady's memory, glittering mountains and lions stalking, an Indian trance dancer, a volcano's pitiless crater. What great riches there are in the world – and I've seen at least some of them before I die. I feel richer – mentally, artistically and spiritually.

Day 85 Manchester, England

At 7.15am I'm awake to see the last shadows of night across Ireland. It looks like fairyland, an inky blue landscape sprinkled with the golden dust of scattered villages. At 7.30am cotton wool clouds puff across the Irish Sea and ahead of me is a pink and gold sunburst of dawn. The slender wing of my aircraft reflects a single beam of light, like a herald of the new day. Finally, we hover over England itself, smothered in cloud and the land below in shadow. It looks industrial, over-populated and busy, even at this early hour. But it's my home.

Returning home — one week later

It's a week now since I sank into Laurence's arms at Arrivals. I'm still overjoyed to be home and enjoying simple pleasures like the delicate frost decorating our village, rediscovering my long-forgotten woolly clothes and taking steaming hot baths. Unpacking my bag for the last time was weird. Some of my clothes were discarded as recently as my stop-off in Hawaii where in desperation at my appearance I bought new T-shirts in a Mall and stuffed old ones in a bin. The rest look pretty raggy. If I did it again I would pack a whole wardrobe of top-quality trekking gear for its strength and quick drying qualities. Amazingly, I managed without a Pacamac and never got wet.

There are deeper changes that coming home also brings about. I want to focus more on my ambitions and to share plans with Laurence about where we are going with our lives. Even after only one month abroad, Laurence has also found a new perspective and clarity about our future. We have had long deep conversations about work and where to live, both having visited the fundamental question: what are we doing with our lives?

After five months travelling without her husband, Susan had learned a great many new skills and a lot about herself. Her feelings about returning the UK were entirely positive:

'It felt good to return. I was ready to be home.'

But for many travellers a reverse culture shock is triggered by the return to a peculiarly unfamiliar Britain. Coming home typically leaves long-term travellers feeling flat and depressed. The contrast between rich and poor can be overwhelming, as Polly found on her return:

'I felt disgusted with the wealth, greed and waste in the west."

Josh expressed his return home as a schizophrenic wrench between a carefree life in Asia and a grim return to the cold British winter:

'Life on the other side seemed cosmopolitan, fun and interesting. Only days before I'd felt the warm sea of a lagoon lapping my toes below the bright blue sky. Then it was coats, gloves and cold grey drizzle. I got blank looks of boredom from people who missed out on my epic journey. The realities returned – no long-term address or job, so loads of hassle. It's like waking from a dream to find you really don't exist and thinking, "Why the hell have I come back?"'

Josh had fallen into a nasty hole in the system due to his having no permanent address or job in the UK and consequently found it difficult to get credit or benefits. Reluctantly, he stayed with a friend who acted as a guarantor for the flat-share he eventually moved to. It took him six months of 'temping and general hell' to get established again in the UK.

On the flight home from her world trip, Sue felt terribly sad that her big adventure was over, despite her pride in the unforgettable experience she had given her two sons:

'On the downside, for me it has been an unsettling experience, mundane everyday life seems monotonous and boring. For the boys this trip has engendered a desire to explore the world further. Surely this must be a good thing. The traditional annual holiday of two weeks in Greece will never be quite the same. In fact I doubt now we will ever do that again.'

After two years in Ghana, Emrys was also disorientated on his return to the UK:

'When I got back I was lost in places like Tesco. I mean, why do you need this much food? Because out there in Ghana a shop has two cans of different things. I was also probably unnecessarily thin

when I came back. But it was very nice to come home and be anonymous, to walk down the street and no kids shouting "obruni!" (white man).'

Linda and James also felt they returned to earth with a hard bump. On a positive note, the house rental to a friend was successful and there were no difficulties with practical issues. However,

LAURA'S TIPS: Home without the hassle

To avoid a re-entry nightmare don't burn your bridges before you leave:

✓ Keep a UK address if at all possible as it is your route to many state benefits and a healthy credit record.

✓ Try to avoid a lapse in registration with your GP or dentist while away.

✓ Keep your UK bank account open and functioning or there may be long delays in reopening accounts when you return.

✓ If you are renting out your home but are forced home early, do you have a contingency plan for a roof over your head?

✓ Always keep some savings to cover unexpected events on your return.

emotionally they had to deal with a recent bereavement and the grind of returning to work:

> 'The benefit of renting our house to someone we knew was that the telephone and internet was all set up and there wasn't a lot of calling around to do. The downside was the small gamble that they didn't overuse the gas or electricity or wreck anything in the house, but we knew the people fairly well. I am not sure what we will do again in the future – it is great having someone you know in the house, and that is probably the easiest and best solution. But emotionally it was depressing. James' grandma died two days before we came home so that was very hard. And since then it has been very hard to settle back to normality. Rather than quelling our desire to travel it has just strengthened it and we are saving so we can go again.'

Fran's return also helped her realise there are things about her life at home she wants to change. One common theme is the need to declutter. After seeing how few possessions many people have, a house full of unnecessary objects can strike many homecomers as excessive.

> 'I suppose coming home was a bit flat really. It was nice to be home but I walked in and I looked at my house and I thought – did I leave it in such a state? And I realised I had far too many possessions. I need to get rid of a lot of stuff. I'm also setting my priorities differently.'

Gilly and Ken had a similar reaction and, like Fran, felt some regrets at not having moved to New Zealand earlier in their lives:

> 'We wished we had emigrated when we were younger. Since coming home we have been decluttering. I was extremely sad to leave New Zealand. There has never been a day when I haven't thought about the people we met, the amazing space and the scenery.'

Reckoning the costs

I've now had time to review my mountain of post including a big pile of credit card and bank statements. The damage after just three months amounts to £4,300. That works out at a rather large £358 per week. It's more than I expected to spend, given that my flight was paid for by my competition win, but I'm not too upset as I can offset some earnings against this. My telecommuting wasn't quite as profitable as I would have hoped but I have kept my contract work bubbling over, contributed to a few magazines and kept a few cheques rolling in from writing. The big bonus has been a whopping £1,000 tax rebate paid straight into my bank account while I was in Indonesia. So in the final reckoning I'm only £1,740 out of pocket. After deducting my earnings and tax rebate the trip has only cost me £145 per week. When I consider where I've been and what I've done, maybe I should take this up full-time.

Travellers' costs

Looking at our group of grown-up travellers, the wide variety of trips is reflected in very different final costs. The cheapest trip cost £1,500 and the most expensive £16,000 per person. Costs per week also varied hugely, from £100 to £1,500 (including all transport costs). While in no way being a scientific sample of grown-up gap travellers, some interesting points emerge about the costs of a long trip. Firstly, the cheaper journeys all involved people taking their own transport or relying on public facilities. Clearly, driving your own campervan or jumping on local trains and buses is going to do wonders for your wallet.

Secondly, the choice of country is a key factor in how much you spend. Africa, Asia and eastern Europe all cost the least to travel around, with many contributors remarking on the cheapness of accommodation. Also getting plenty of feedback was the high cost of travelling in a few countries, notably in Australia and Japan. To really bring the cost down, the combination of public transport and a cheap country should be a winner – but there was plenty of anecdotal evidence that this was just too hot, sweaty and tiring for the majority. Once in a developing country most travellers opted for cut-price locally organised tours that allowed them to relax and take in the sights rather than get too involved in bus and train timetables.

Working your passage is undoubtedly the best way to keep costs down. Emrys received a small stipend for his charity work and says he 'just made a tiny loss over two years'. Only the two youngest travellers were eligible to work on Australia's Working Holiday Scheme. Both significantly cut their outgoings and were also enthusiastic about the other benefits of working. In Paul's case his high-grade IT skills all but paid for his year away. George earned less but enthused about the contacts and experiences he gained in Sydney.

Whether to take organised tours or the independent route is absolutely clear cut when considering cost. All-inclusive tours can easily double or triple your outlay. Yet in many countries, tours are by far the quickest and most comfortable way to get around. In a few countries the only way to enter is on a group visa, so signing up for a tour is compulsory.

Finally, unlike typical backpackers, a number of our contributors flew business class for health and comfort reasons. Paying as much as £6,000 for a business class flight is way beyond the dreams of the average gap traveller but some of our older travellers put a reclining seat and extra space at a premium when flying around the globe.

What is also apparent is that the budget seems to bear little relation to how much enjoyment our travellers recorded. Spending a small fortune will naturally guarantee greater comfort and protection from the harsher rigours of travel. But there is no evidence that those who spent most had a better trip or were guaranteed protection from illness or accidents.

The benefits

The best bits for me were about sharing – being part of a group in the wonderful Maasai Mara, tracing my family history with my sisters, showing my son his roots and being with Laurence in the great outdoors of New Zealand. Meeting other people while travelling was also fascinating and staying at homestays certainly gave me the most potent taste of local foods and lifestyles. The conversations I was lucky enough to have gave me unforgettable insights into other people's lives – so different from me yet so like me in their essential hopes and concerns.

I'm not alone in finding the biggest benefit for me is a new sense of confidence. I may have been a bit wobbly at times but I'm stronger because I did it – I went around the world at 46, largely on my own, and I survived to tell the tale. I feel braver, more tolerant and much, much more aware of the world and its marvels. I feel truly privileged to have seen the landscapes and wonders that I have. It's been the perfect mid-life experience and I've returned feeling physically and mentally stronger.

Personal change

A long time away will inevitably mean you aren't quite the same person opening your front door after a period of months or a year. More enlightened, tolerant, and confident are the ways most travellers say they have changed. For many it brings about a profound re-evaluation of how they are living their lives and what to do next. For those still working it can be a time to radically

---

What do you wish you had known before you set off?

'How much fun we were going to have. I would have planned a much longer trip.' Sue

'I think part of the beauty of travelling is being surprised by things.' Emrys

'That it is easy to buy whatever you want wherever you want.' Kate and Keith

'That easy access to savings at home is always useful in case of emergencies.' Joanne

'To worry less about what 'may' happen and the unknown.' Josh

'I can't thing of anything. We enjoy spontaneity and surprise.' Gilly and Ken

'How hard it would be to come home.' James and Linda

---

reconsider how to earn a living and use talents that have been stimulated by travel:

> *'I've come back feeling that I don't want to live a routine existence. I've had so many wonderful adventures and seen such treasures that I've decided I want to work abroad – perhaps teaching English or travel writing.'* Abby

After travelling extensively through Asia and east Asia, Josh also changed his approach to work after returning to London:

> *'I didn't even bother looking for a permanent job. Thanks to the local Business Link I've started my own personal training business*

and am attempting to live my dream of freedom over here. I also import eastern health goods and sell them for profit thanks to my new contacts. Success is up to me and my wits, not some faceless company holding me back.'

For Kate and Keith, it's not just their approach to work that has changed. They have returned to their native north-east and are currently happily renting a house after collecting some of their old possessions from friends. Kate is working two days a week at her old job while Keith is working on sculptures in a local quarry. But their values and beliefs have been fundamentally altered by their year away:

'What we have done, by selling everything and going away, is given ourselves a fresh start. It's an opportunity to think – what are we going to do with the next 30 years of our lives? We are also no longer feeling the fear of 'what if I loose my footing on the property ladder, what about my pension? Fear results in self-limiting behaviour.'

By contrast, Ajay has recently retired from general practice and is celebrating his complete freedom to travel. But his time spent abroad has also sparked a keen desire to continue to use his medical skills in the service of less-fortunate people:

'I now open a new chapter of a different life, a life in which every day is a Sunday. There is much more to life than writing out prescriptions for penicillin from morning to night. I can now indulge in my hobby of travelling round the world and off the beaten track. Of course I won't be giving up medicine altogether. I am going to combine medicine with charity work. What I have in mind is to open a primary care/health education centre in one of the poorer countries of Africa and work for three months a year. The countries I have in mind are Burkina Faso, Mali and Niger. They don't have industry or natural resources to blip on the inter-

national radar screen. People are dirt poor. So three months a year will be devoted there.'

After returning home early from Australia, Joanne at first felt rather deflated by the weather. But she soon realised events had worked out in her favour:

'After all the build-up to get back to my boyfriend Mark, it was a bit flat really. It was also February, very dark and cold and I now missed my son George as he'd stayed on to work in Sydney. I couldn't win! But I loved getting back to clean ant-free sheets and some of my personal things, especially my laptop. In any case I soon moved house to live with Mark. We are now married so it all worked out beautifully. George and I had shared the experience of our lives and closed a phase of my life just before starting another very happy one for me.'

Not coming home

For George, the trip that had been prompted by his dissatisfaction with work in London also led to a dramatic change of life. Eight months after his mother left Australia his working visa expired and he followed her home for a few months:

'I had changed but home hadn't. It reminded me of how a time traveller would feel after arriving back from a wonderful adventure, with no one understanding what he had experienced. Once your awareness has been raised, a trip or experience will change a part of you forever. This led me to apply for residence and migrating. I have now set up my own property business, live in Sydney and am currently looking forward to a holiday in the Pacific islands – something I could never have imagined doing a few years ago.'

Career gapper Paul also found the return to Britain impossible after a gap year of freedom:

'Pandora's Box had been opened and it would be difficult to close it. My life could never be the same again. In Australia I'd worked in a technical/IT-based role. It paid well, allowed me to gain more experience in my career and contributed points towards my over-all residency application. I now live in laid-back Perth, Australia, and have a dual passport, so it's clearly changed my life.'

It's not only the younger gappers who have taken the plunge to make their gap year permanent. At 54, Tim also felt uninspired to stay in the UK after his 'mid-life adventure' in Morocco:

'Coming home made me feel sad, but happy with the change in me. Within 24 hours I was more determined than ever to get out of here and get back. I had to come home to sort out various family and financial affairs. That done, I am going back, have a job to go to out there and enough cash to buy a small house.

'The trip was what I needed. When the kids have left home and the mortgage is paid off, or easy, there is a change for everybody. For some it's a seamless change, like an automatic gearbox on a car. Mine needed a kick-start and some nifty gear changes with double de-clutching. I now have a new focus, a new slant on life and a much more positive outlook. Wealth has passed me by (or been squandered) but health and the pursuit of happiness are there to be taken.'

Tim was last heard of en route to the Pyrenees on his way back to Morocco, where he is intending to work in property sales.

A world of opportunity

The trend for longer and more adventurous holidays continues. This year's slogan is '60 is the new 40' and advances in healthcare mean more and more of us will retain our fitness well into our 60s, 70s and 80s. To help plan our travels we have the internet with its near-infinite amount of information on every part of the globe. Dismissive terms like 'saga louts' or 'denture adventurers' miss the point. These trips are a wonderful opportunity for us all to be enriched by the beauty and uniqueness of the world. No longer mere consumers of holiday packages, many older travellers are sensitive to their destinations and keen to befriend locals and put cash into local economies.

And what about you? I do hope that reading these accounts has inspired you to forge your own route and see the world. The time has never been better to discover new places and explore the great natural wonders of the world. Flights are getting cheaper, work-places are allowing more of us to take career breaks and tour operators offer a multitude of fascinating tours on every subject from tribal treks in Thailand to art appreciation in Tuscany. Or perhaps you've been inspired to take the independent route and plot your own way, finding accommodation and adventure off the beaten track.

Whatever you choose, take a lesson from the band of travellers who contributed to this book. A long trip away is more than a holiday. Being away from home and family gives ample time for reflection and refreshment. Only one thing is guaranteed. Travel with an open mind and you will change for the better and be enriched forever.

Final words from our travellers

"If it is to be, it is up to me' – 10 little words, each two letters long, with such a big meaning.' Tim

'Don't think – do it. It's no use having your heart's yearn and not going out to do it. You won't be here forever.' Fran

'Just go for it and be careful.' Sue

'I did things I didn't know I could do.' Polly

'If you don't look, you won't find.' Michael and Mary-Ann

'It's part of the spirit of the age – I went out and did my bit.' Emrys

'Go before the world changes forever.' Charles and Elize

'Age is no barrier to seeing the world in its incredible variety.' Joanne

'Time is marching on – better now than never.' Gilly and Ken

'It was a great way to strengthen our marriage.' James and Linda

'My trip was like a seed that fell on concrete and became a glorious garden.' George

'Take a gap year to see what opportunities are out there – and you may find a few surprises on the way.' Josh

'The world is out there to see and experience.' Ajay

'You've read this book – now book your own trip!' Laura